Christoph Stückelberger   **Global Trade Ethics**

Christoph Stückelberger

Global Trade Ethics
An Illustrated Overview

With a preface by Rubens Ricupero, UNCTAD

WCC Publications
Geneva

The author, Christoph Stückelberger, is general secretary of the development agency *Bread for All* (Switzerland) and professor of ethics at the Theological Faculty of the University of Basel.

Address of the author: Allenmoosstrasse 66, CH-8057 Zurich
e-mail: stueckelberger@swissonline.ch
http://www.christophstueckelberger.ch

Thanks to *Bread for All*, Berne, for its contribution to the publication of this book.

Translated from the German by Tony Häfliger and Vivien Blandford

Cover design and layout: Atelier Mühlberg, Basel

ISBN 2-8254-1369-0

© 2002, WCC Publications, World Council of Churches
150 route de Ferney, P. O. Box 2100
1211 Geneva 2, Switzerland
http://www.wcc-coe.org

Imprimé en France par Imprimerie Lienhart - Aubenas
N° d'imprimeur : 5465

Contents

Preface

A book on global trade ethics could not come at a more appropriate time. Indeed, at this early juncture in the new century, there is an increased realization that the economy in general, and trade in particular, cannot be insulated from moral and spiritual values. Eleven such fundamental values form the ethical basis for global trade in Christoph Stückelberger's book (see the second chapter). Unlike astronomical or physical phenomena such as the movement of planets, the economy is not governed by laws that are independent of human will and decision-making. On the contrary, economic conditions are the result of societal forces and policy choices based, at least implicitly, on a set of beliefs and values. There thus exists a margin for manoeuvre within society, particularly for policy makers, to give sense and meaning to economic activity – albeit within the limits imposed by such constraints as the availability of capital, labour, material resources and technological knowledge. The economy, in other words, should not and indeed cannot be disentangled from all other aspects of social and cultural life.

This being the case, how can one explain the hegemony of the economy in today's world? In a book called *Une société en quête de sens*, Jean-Baptiste DE FOUCAULD and Denis PIVETEAU have attempted to provide an explanation based on the assumption that the role of the economy in society has gone through three phases. In the first, in traditional, pre-industrial society, the economy was relatively controlled, worked in a non-autonomous way and was integrated into a broader system. In the second stage, in industrial society, the economy acquired greater autonomy, although it kept its fundamental meaning which was to reduce scarcity and increase welfare. In the third phase, that of today, the economy has gained ascendancy over politics, society and human beings. Everything around it is effaced: religion has lost its relevance, the great political-revolutionary ideologies have fallen apart and all the other systems capable of imparting meaning to social life have vanished. The market economy thus threatens to generate a "market society" where everything is for sale.

A curious phenomenon then emerges: the economy itself begins to lose its original meaning, the reduction of scarcity and the increase in welfare. On the one hand, for the fortunate, there is no longer a scarcity of basic goods such as food or clothing. Consumerism has to invent new needs, ever more superfluous. On the other hand, and in order to maintain the necessary conditions for this excessive accumulation, the new economy starts to threaten or to destroy the welfare of growing sectors of the population previously protected by a reasonable degree of job security and by social insurance. The economy no longer contains much meaning, but neither is there much meaning to be found outside it.

There results a sort of imperialistic domination of the economy over other fields, thus subverting the harmony of the *Spheres of Justice* postulated by Michael WALZER in his book of the same title. For this American political philosopher, there should be not one single principle of justice but several, each applicable to a different sphere of the pluralistic human community. In each sphere, there is a specific good that is sought by all: money in the economic sphere of the market, power in the field of politics and government, leisure in the world of entertainment, knowledge in the sphere of education, love in the universe of the family, etc. A small group always tends to monopolize the central good of each sphere, but the greatest danger occurs whenever one of those spheres becomes predominant. When this happens, the masters of the market, for example, may use their advantage in order to control goods particular to other spheres, thereby becoming also the rulers of power, knowledge or leisure. The best way to avoid the encroachment of one sphere onto the others and to maintain a healthy autonomy and balance among them is for the state to make effective use of its active function of social regulation.

One of the spheres in which the neglect of ethical imperatives has become unacceptable is that of trade. We are indeed witnessing dramatic imbalances in world trade relations, where power and knowledge are being manipulated by a few, thus undermining the prospects for large segments of humanity to overcome poverty and achieve minimum standards of well-being.

A fourth phase in the evolution of the role of the economy in society needs to replace the current one, striking the right balance between economic and ethical values. International trade will probably be the pivotal instrument in this process because of its role in making national economies and societies global. Nowadays, trade is a vehicle of values that are profoundly altering the nature of relations among societies and cultures. The interplay between trade policies and international trade rules is evolving towards sophisticated legal mechanisms that bind the behaviour of governments, firms, citizens and communities. Being at the crossroads of several key policy areas – development strategies, labour policies, cultural trends, transfer of technology – trade rules are a sphere in which the need to harmonize economic, social and ethical values is becoming increasingly imperative.

By way of example, less than 10 years ago it would have been unthinkable for international trade negotiations to have considered the role of governments in shaping national education systems. But when discussing the modalities of negotiations on audiovisual and cultural services in the framework of the negotiations on trade in services, this is precisely what is now at stake. The concerns about local languages, cultures and knowledge that need "protection" against globalizing forces are being upgraded to the level of high strategic goals in the trade fora. Similarly, any international rule regarding trade in professional services, such as nursing, is now being seen as affecting, for example, the health systems of developing and developed countries alike.

The recent impassioned debate taking place at the World Trade Organization (WTO) in particular on intellectual property and access to medicines, is clearly a case of clashing policy areas where the international community has to formulate a "code of conduct" that balances the interests of research with those of health, and where ethical considerations will loom large in the corresponding policy-making. At the November 2001 WTO Conference in Doha, Qatar, a positive result was achieved in this area by the adoption, in a ministerial declaration, of clear principles with regard to trade in medicines and public health: the Doha declaration recognizes and endorses the right of developing countries to obtain essential drugs without necessarily having to pay the onerous prices normally allowed under patent protection.

Ethics-related considerations, however, might sometimes be used as criteria for disguised protectionism. Environmental and food security concerns, for example, might be misused as a means of averting trade liberalization concessions in the field of agriculture. Environmental conservation and food security are undoubtedly critical objectives that need to be pursued, yet rules must ensure that they will not be utilized to avoid opening the markets of industrialized countries to agricultural exports originating in developing countries.

Through trade, the role of governments in defining the borders and the content of "public goods" and "public policies" is being modified and subjected to new international rules. In fact, by transmitting such values as development, employment, participation in the benefits of global growth, poverty reduction and technology, trade itself should be considered as a "public good" for the international community. This is probably the main value that remains to be ensured through international codes: the effective and equitable participation of developing countries in the multilateral trading system is a "development value" for these countries. Correcting the imbalances that characterize the trading system is therefore a major challenge in the process of identifying rules that balance economic with other social values. That process is still very young and incomplete. Let us hope that it will evolve towards a new holistic system of international values and rules, in which economic, social, cultural and development needs are given due consideration and duly realized. Christoph Stückelberger's book on Global Trade Ethics makes an important contribution to these efforts towards a new holistic system. His ethical vision and practical proposals for future-oriented ethical instruments in global trade give orientation and hope.

Rubens Ricupero
Secretary-General
UNCTAD

Introduction

The globalization of the world economy is characterized by rapidly increasing trade across international borders. Globalized trade arouses great hopes of expanding prosperity and progress in the fight against world poverty; at the same time, however, globalization reinforces resistance to, and fear of, relentless international competition, marginalization and new instances of poverty. This is the tension within which we seek creative approaches to an ethically responsible arrangement of trade at the global, national, corporate and individual levels.

This book introduces the ethics of trade by raising topical, ethical questions in the context of this field of tension, revealing existing and potential approaches to the solution of these questions. It further intends to provide methodological bearings to help readers form their own ethical judgments and name ethical instruments and agents so as to identify specific ways out of a state of helplessness. The goal of the book is to arouse hope and demonstrate that ethical action is indeed possible. Many aspects of this method may be applied to other areas of business ethics beyond the sphere of trade.

Although intentionally ethical investments constitute roughly 0.1% of all the investments worldwide, this book aims to demonstrate that ethics is not merely a "point one percent phenomenon" of concern only to idealists situated on the margins of the economy. Ethics is part and parcel of the core business of the economy and its agents.

The book's focus is primarily on aspects of business ethics, but secondarily it is on aspects of economic policy and the macro-economy. It reveals immediate opportunities for action by companies (particularly with regard to foreign trade) and in civil society, but it also examines the actions necessary for the creation of national and international trade policies.

The content of this book is predicated on theologically informed business ethics. Christian values and their distortions have shaped the development of Western economies to a crucial extent and are still capable of providing some direction today. However, in these pages ethical priorities and value judgments are usually formulated without any specific reference to theological premises and grounds.[1] Thus, these ethical priorities and value judgments regarding globalized trade may be understood from various ideological perspectives.

The systemic framework for business ethics is the market economy. Extensive discussion of fundamental models and alternatives to this economic system is beyond the scope of the present work. The instruments of ethical business proposed here refer to a socially and ecologically responsible economy that may be regulated where the need arises.

The target audience for this book is made up of people with leadership responsibilities and other members of staff of trading companies and other firms, fair trade organizations, governmental offices (particularly those involved in international policy and development), non-governmental organizations, international organizations, institutions directly addressing questions of ethics, churches and students of economics, theology and ethics.

1   For such premises and grounds, please refer to the author's other publications in the field of ethics, particularly *Umwelt und Entwicklung*, Stuttgart, 1997.

Reading aid

The reader may begin the book anywhere. Virtually every double page treats a self-contained topic with a table or illustration on the left and an explanatory text on the right. Chapters 1–3 provide the basics of ethics, and chapters 4–6 show the instruments, agents and applied fields of action necessary for ethical trade. It is recommended that chapter 3 be read before chapters 4–6 for better comprehension of the principles of ethical valuation.

Basics I
Ethics in trade

To begin with, trade ethics as a part of business ethics raises questions of introductory clarification: What exactly is ethics? What does it comprise? What does trade as a central part of the economy comprise? What are its mechanisms, agents and institutions? And what, actually, are the ethical aspects of trade action? What is the specific contribution of trade ethics towards the whole of present-day business ethics? What kind of trade in the globalized world on the threshold of the 21st century are we looking at? What specific intentions are behind the various terms of ethically responsible trade?

Questions such as these are clarified in this introductory chapter so as to demonstrate the bandwidth of these aspects and, at the same time, allow for a more precise formulation of the problems involved.

Specific domains of ethics

Health ethics
Medical ethics
Sexual ethics
Bioethics

Life-form ethics
Marital and family ethics
Ethnic communities
Intergenerational ethics

Resources ethics
Ethics of the bases of life
Animal ethics
Biodiversity ethics

Corporate ethics
Labor ethics
Ethics of economic systems
Trade ethics
Consumer ethics
Professional ethics

Legal ethics
Ethics of political systems
Peace ethics
Land ethics

Media ethics
Sports ethics
Cultural ethics
Ethics of religions

Main domains of ethics

Life ethics

Community ethics

Environmental ethics

Business ethics

Political ethics

Cultural/religious ethics

Types of ethics

Meta-ethics

Normative ethics

Descriptive ethics

Ethics
Acting responsibly in all spheres of life

© Stückelberger: Global Trade Ethics

Ethics and morals

Ethics strives to answer questions such as: What should I do? How should I act? How should a community of people act? Thus ethics concerns all areas of life (→ graph on the left) to the extent to which a human being can and must decide in favour of one or two or more courses of action. Ethics strives to answer the question as to what is good and just action. It strives to provide signposts for responsible action in all areas of life. It does so with comprehensible methods and steps (→ ch. 2.3) and, depending on the ethical approach, on various philosophical, religious and ideological grounds (→ ch. 2.2). *Morals* – a term that tends to have pejorative connotations these days – represent the basic framework of rules for action, standards of value and fundamental ideas that are prevalent in a society and manifest themselves in its customs and manners.

Three forms of ethics

1. *Descriptive or empirical ethics* describes the diverse manifestations of existing morals and customs of individuals, groups, peoples, institutions and cultures.
2. *Normative ethics* subjects existing morals to a critical examination and formulates standards from which action should take its bearings. It does so on the basis of a certain ethical approach.
3. *Meta-ethics* critically examines the ethical methods themselves and develops them further.

In this book, the main emphasis is on normative ethics. Meta-ethics and descriptive ethics will be mentioned only marginally.

The six main domains of ethics

Life ethics concerns itself with the beginning, preservation and end of life. The *ethics of community forms* deals with issues of communal life. Environmental ethics examines aspects of people's relationships with their non-human environment. *Business ethics* focuses on the production of, trade in, consumption and disposal of goods and services. Political ethics looks into questions of the interaction of national communities and groups of people through political institutions. *Cultural and religious ethics* is concerned with action and communal life through the medium of cultural and religious institutions.

3

1.2 Trade: Definition and scope

Areas of trade

Tariff regulations
Protective measures
Technical trade barriers
Investment measures
Origin regulations
Goods dispatch regulations
Import licence procedures
Payment regulations
Government procurement
Anti-corruption laws
Service regulations
Competition law
International environ-
ment law
etc.

Financing
Personnel
Investment
Material economy
Production
Marketing
Leadership
Organization
Accounting
Information manage-
ment law
etc.

Labour law
Shop closing laws
Fiscal policy
Competition law
Brand laws
Subsidies
etc.

Foreign trade policy	Business administration	Domestic trade policy

Foreign trade	Domestic trade

Trade

Agriculture (forestry, fisheries) Primary sector	Services Trade Tertiary sector	Industry/ small business Secondary sector

Economy

Global Trade Ethics focuses on ethical questions of foreign trade. Many criteria, however, also apply to domestic trade.

© Stückelberger: Global Trade Ethics

Definition of trade

Trade is basically the exchange of economic goods. We speak of "trade in a functional sense" if participants in the market procure goods from or sell goods to others which they do not produce or process themselves (merchandise). In practice, the term is generally restricted to the exchange of material goods, and even more frequently to the exchange of movable material goods.

Functions of trade

- Goods turnover (from producer-oriented to demand-oriented; i.e. influence of purchase as regards place, time, duration, situation).
- Adaptation to demand (connection of material supply and services, including goods and monetary logistics).
- Support in seeking the decision to purchase (through information about goods and indications of alternative action).
- Market equalization (settlement between supply and demand).
- Processing of material goods (sorting, adaptation, installation, after-sales service and support).

An increase in labour output produces more trade. World trade is growing at about 2.5 times the rate of the global production of material goods.

Types of goods in exchange relations

1. *Nominal goods:* claims to real goods (money, securities).
2. *Real goods:*
   2.1 Material goods
      2.1.1 Durable goods (real estate)
      2.1.2 Utility goods (plant, machinery, equipment)
      2.1.3 Turnover goods (raw materials, accessory materials, materials, goods, finished goods)
   2.2 Rights (patents, licences, water rights, etc.)
   2.3 Services (in transport, forwarding, storage, insurance, brokerage, etc.)

Domestic trade and foreign trade are two fundamental forms of trade. Foreign trade is increasing in significance owing to globalization; however, domestic trade remains important and is often underestimated.

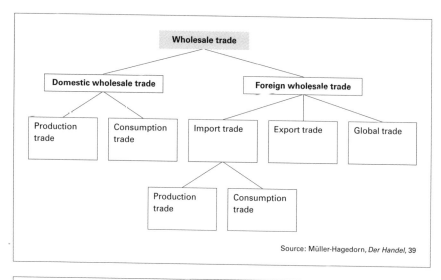

Source: Müller-Hagedorn, *Der Handel*, 39

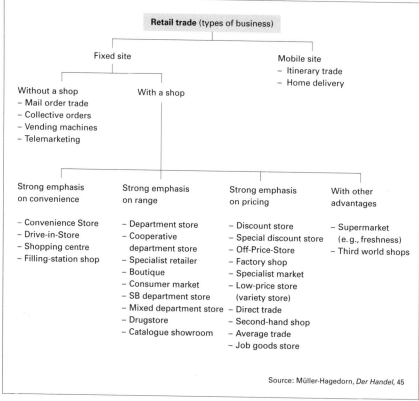

Source: Müller-Hagedorn, *Der Handel*, 45

Types of trading companies and institutions

The German Committee for Terminological Definitions in Trade and Marketing defines the institutional aspect of trade as follows: "Trade in its institutional sense – also called a trading company, a trading operation or a shop – includes institutions whose economic activity must exclusively or predominantly be ascribed to trade in the functional sense. Official statistics classify a company or operation under trade if its trading activities produce more added value than its secondary or other activities."

In reality, however, an increasing number of companies combine and mix production, trade and other activities so that the borderlines become blurred (→ chs. 5.4–7). This also makes for an increase in the conflicts between trade and industry, and has resulted in the demand for new partnerships (BRABECK/NESTLÉ 2000).

Three groups of institutions which engage in trade

a) *Companies*

b) The *state* (territorial entities and social insurance)

c) *Private households* and *non-profit organizations*

The four important operational forms of trade

a) *Retail trade* is an operation whereby someone sells merchandise to private households on his own or a third party's account.

b) *Wholesale trade* is an operation whereby someone sells merchandise to a purchaser other than a private household on his own or a third party's account.

c) *Brokerage* is an operation whereby someone arranges for the purchase and sale of merchandise for a third party's account.

d) *Combined systems* integrate retail or wholesale organizations into the corporate policy of companies by means of sustained relations, franchizing being a case in point. Such systems produce synergies and dependencies for individual operations.

Levels of action for business ethics

Environmental ethics

Institutional ethics

Personal ethics

Individual ethics

Professional ethics

Management ethics

Business ethics

Ethics of domestic trade policy

Ethics of foreign trade policy

Ethics of environmental trade policy

Business administration according to functions (cf. Thommen 1996, 52)	Business ethics according to areas (Stückelberger)
Basic functions:	*Basic functions:*
Financing	Financing ethics
Investment	Investment ethics
Material management	Material management ethics
Production	Production ethics
Marketing	Marketing ethics
Cross-sectional functions:	*Cross-sectional functions:*
Management	Management ethics
Personnel	Personnel ethics
Organization	Organization ethics
Accounting	Accounting ethics
Information management	Information management ethics
Law	Law ethics

Four levels of ethical action

Ethical action takes place immediately and mediately; i.e., mediated by structures. A distinction may be made between four levels:

- *Individual ethics* concerns individuals' immediate action with reference to themselves or their fellow human beings (I–I, I–you).
- *Personal ethics* concerns persons' immediate action within or between groups (we–you).
- *Institutional ethics*, also called *structural ethics* or frequently *social ethics*, concerns mediate action: here, standards are provided by structures such as institutions, systems, or laws. Individual action is strongly influenced by this. People are able to modify these structures (I/we–it/structure).
- *Environmental ethics* concerns people's mediate or immediate action with reference to the non-human environment (I/we–nature).

Domains of trade ethics

Every domain of ethics (→ ch. 1.1) and thus also of business ethics and trade ethics as part of the latter, has to do with all four levels of ethical action. This results in the *matrix* of the graph on the left. In trade ethics, a distinction can be made between the following sub-domains (this list is not exhaustive):

- *Professional ethics* covers people's responsibility at work from their choice of an occupation to the way they pursue and modify it, until retirement, and all the relationships connected with this; the family is an example. The focus is on individual and personal ethics.
- *Management ethics* covers the management of a company, particularly with reference to employees and citizens. This involves all four levels of ethical action, with individual and personal ethics being particularly important.
- *Business ethics* covers all areas of corporate activity (jobs, product quality, logistics, advertising, marketing, transport, choice of trading partners and countries, etc.). All four levels of ethics are involved, with structural ethics being of particular importance.
- *The ethics of domestic trade policy and of foreign trade policy* cover all the issues of economic policy at a macro level, which predominantly involves structural and environmental ethics.
- *The ethics of trade/environment policy* chiefly covers the impact of trade on the environment and is thus concerned with environmental ethics.

	Production	Purchase	Sale	Consumption	Disposal
What?	Need-oriented? Market-oriented? Plan-oriented?	Product-range planning? Producer-/country-orientation?	Product-range planning? Brand/label policy?	Consumer-oriented? Demand-oriented?	Disposal planned in production? Recycling possible?
How much?	Need-oriented? Market-oriented? Plan-oriented?	Turnover-/profit-oriented? Concentration process?	Turnover-/profit-oriented? Concentration process?	Health- and sustainability-oriented?	Minimized disposal volume?
Where? By whom?	Appropriate to location? Investment policy poverty-oriented?	From producer? Intermediate trade? Its values and standards?	Type of sale? Shop concepts?	Household? Mobile consumption? Other sites of consumption?	Appropriate to location? Close to consumption?
How?	Production methods? Working conditions? Wages?	Transport methods? Working conditions? Wages? Prices?	Marketing? Adverts? Working conditions? Wages? Prices?	Consumer information/advice? Label-oriented?	Sustainable, save? Internalized external costs?
When?	Production time proper and humane?	Delivery time proper and humane?	Shop opening hours? Working hours?	Humane and environmentally sound?	In time and sustainable?
For whom?	Poverty-oriented? Fair distribution?	Poverty-oriented? Fair distribution?	Poverty-oriented? Fair distribution?	Poverty-oriented? Fair distribution?	Causation principle observed?

© Stückelberger: Global Trade Ethics

Fundamental questions of economic and trade ethics

■ *What should be produced and traded in?*
  What goods and services are necessary for the world's six billion people to live in dignity (fundamental need orientation)? What goods and services are produced because there is purchasing power and a market for them (demand orientation)?

■ *How much should be produced and traded?*
  A volume has a decisive impact on the price, but also on the globalization and concentration processes of production and trade. What measure is ethically optimal? What cultural, world political and religious consequences have the coercive power to increase volumes?

■ *Where and by whom should production and trade be conducted?*
  The global production of goods is unevenly distributed. Africa's share in global trade is less than 2%. The ethical question addresses the possibility of a fair balance in terms of output, need and distribution (→ ch. 3.2)

■ *How should production and trade be conducted?*
  How should production methods, working conditions, wages, effects on the environment and (peace) policies be ethically judged? Apart from product quality, to what extent are production method issues relevant to trade or not (according to a WTO majority view, they are non-trade concerns)?

■ *When should production and trade be conducted?*
  The way the "production factor time" is treated is highly significant in ethical terms, not only for the just-in-time concept.

■ *For whom should production and trade be conducted?*
  How should target groups defined in the goods and service chain be judged in ethical terms? Is the production of goods and services poverty-oriented, wealth-oriented, middle-class-oriented, women-oriented or ethically, politically or religiously oriented?

These questions apply to the whole "life cycle" of products and services, from planning to the procurement of raw materials, production, purchase, transport, sales and consumption to final disposal. Some of these issues, albeit not all of them by any means, will be introduced to the readers of this book, particularly in chapters 4–6.

Growth of world trade and worldwide production 1950–1998

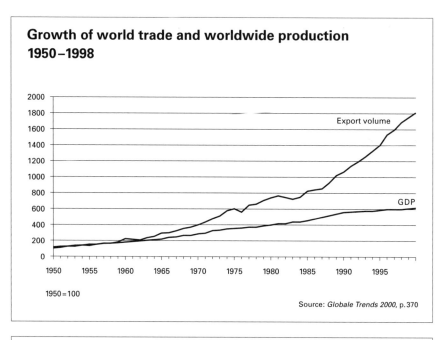

1950 = 100

Source: *Globale Trends 2000*, p. 370

The development of technology shapes the development of trade

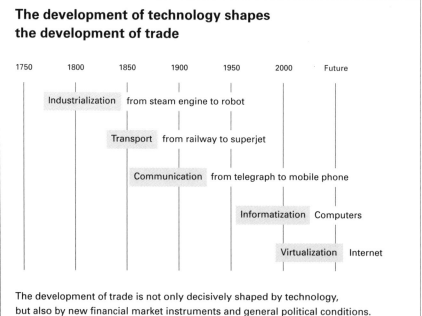

The development of trade is not only decisively shaped by technology, but also by new financial market instruments and general political conditions.

Technical and political factors of development

The general political conditions between liberalization and protectionism of cross-border goods exchange are fundamental to the history of trade. Equally, however, the development of trade has been shaped by the development of technologies (→ graph on the left), of financial instruments and minority policies (minorities that have been forced into trade). The conclusion of purchasing agreements in the exchange of goods involves transaction costs. A trading operation is a transaction cost specialist (MÜLLER, 1998, 125). Technologies and financial instruments have a crucial impact on transaction costs. Trade ethics is therefore also an ethical reflection of technologies (→ ch. 4.10, e-commerce) and financial markets (→ chs. 6.14–16) that have an influence on trade.

Religious and ethical factors of development

Religious and ethical factors have had a crucial effect on world trade again and again. The great international "trading tribes" – Anglo-Saxons, Chinese, Jews, Indians and Japanese – have always been profoundly influenced by the fundamental values of their religions (→ ch. 6.20; KOTKIN 1996). The Old Testament ban on interest, which was in force into the Middle Ages, had as great an impact on trade as the fact that it was lifted by Calvin, who did so on the basis of ethical rules (→ ch. 6.3).

Ethical trade has a long tradition

Although traders traditionally had a bad moral reputation in many cultures, the quest for ethically responsible trade is as old as trade itself (→ next chapter). Often, individual personalities and trading firms fought for this. The battle for fairness in trade also accompanied colonial trade, despite its exploitative practices. One example will suffice: the Basel Trading Society, which evolved from the Basel Mission and traded in the colonies, formulated in its memorandum of association as early as 1859 that its object was "training people in fair-trade practices", which was recalled by Switzerland's ambassador to Ghana in 2000 (P. SCHWEIZER, 2000, p. 102).

Trade in the Ancient Orient 2500 years ago

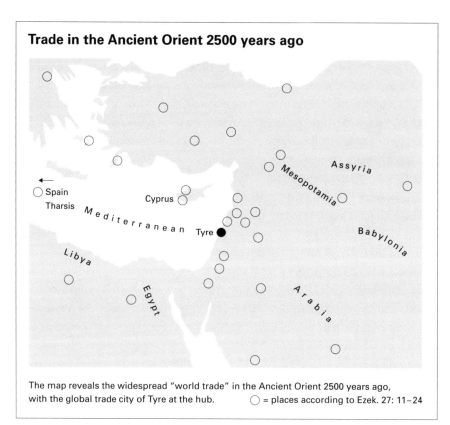

The map reveals the widespread "world trade" in the Ancient Orient 2500 years ago, with the global trade city of Tyre at the hub. ◯ = places according to Ezek. 27: 11–24

The ancient silk route between the Mediterranean and China

(from the 2nd century B.C.)

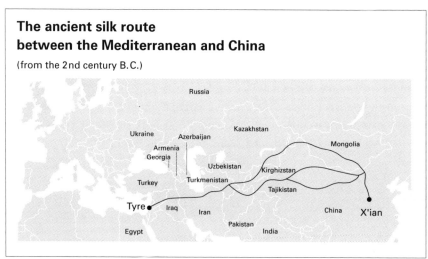

© Stückelberger: Global Trade Ethics

Tyre – a global trade centre: from flourishing trade …

The Phoenician city of Tyre, with its two ports on the Eastern rim of the Mediterranean, was one of the major trade centres in the times of the Old Testament (OT). The main period of long-distance trade lasted from the second half of the 8th century to the first half of the 6th century BC. From Tyre, trade routes led deep into the Arabian heartland and as far as China, North Africa, Spain and the Mediterranean islands. Even in the ancient Orient, long-distance trade produced prosperity and growth. The prophet Ezekiel worked in exile in Babylon from about 597 to 571 BC. He interpreted Tyre's trade in theological terms. The Book of Ezekiel (27:3–28:19) in the OT details the goods and trade routes and praises them in all their splendour. In 585–573 BC, the city had to capitulate before Nebuchadnezzar II, and in 332 BC, it was conquered and razed by Alexander the Great. Chapter 27 bemoans the sinking of the grand ship of Tyre and names two causes for the decline of flourishing trade. First, the king, owing to his trade successes, turned himself into God: "thine heart is lifted up because of thy riches … thou has set thine heart as the heart of God" (28: 5–6). Second, the king abuses his trading power for the purpose of exploitation: "By the multitude of thy merchandise they have filled the midst of thee with violence, and thou hast sinned" (28:16).

… to oppression …

King Solomon, too, was a trader. He owed his power partially to his policy of occupying significant trade routes and controlling them by military means (2 Kings, 10:15). This confirms the natural affirmation of world trade, i. e. long-distance trade that goes beyond domestic trade; it also indicates Solomon's dangerous proximity to pure power politics. Trade agreements were a matter of course even in the times of the OT, for instance between Israel's King Ahab and Damascus (1 Kings 20:34). The slave trade, an offshoot of trade proper, particularly from Tyre, was heavily criticized in the prophetic tradition: "You have sold the people of Judah and Jerusalem to the Greeks, removing them far from their own border." (Joel 3: 6). Tyre "delivered up the whole captivity to Edom" (Amos 1:9). Moreover, there is criticism in the OT that profits are made particularly from trade and do not sufficiently accrue to producers. The merchants of Tyre's neighbouring trading city, Sidon, also brought home riches: "And by the great waters the seed of Sihor, the harvest of the river, is her revenue" (Isa. 23:3).

... and fair trade

After the destruction of the trade metropolis of Tyre – according to the prophet Isaiah – there will be opportunity for fairer trade. Tyre's "merchandise and her hire shall be holiness to the Lord: it shall not be treasured nor laid up; for her merchandise shall be for them that dwell before the Lord, to eat sufficiently ..." (Isa. 23:18).

Jesus: overthrown merchant tables by the Temple

In the New Testament (NT), trade is regarded as a matter of course as much as in the OT. The NT's appeal to change our ways means turning towards God and to the justice of God's kingdom. It is in this *spiritual* perspective – in the sense of a perspective that is oriented towards God and thus towards fellow human beings in a new manner – that Jesus's casting out of the money-changers from the Temple, which is reported in all four gospels (Matt. 21:12 par), may have to be seen. In this manner, Jesus directs trade back to its justified but also limited position on the way towards liberation and salvation. Once the view of God and the kingdom of justice is no longer obstructed by the merchants' tables, trade may again be an instrument in the service of justice.

The *prophetic* call for fair trade is renewed in the Epistle of James: "The wages of the labourers who mowed your fields, which you kept back by fraud, cry out, and the cries of the harvesters have reached the ears of the Lord of hosts." (James 5,4)

Trade is always seen in the *eschatological* perspective – i.e., the perspective that takes into account the final things – of the coming kingdom of God. The parable of the money placed into trust until the return of the king (Luke 19:11–27) makes this appeal: "Do business with them until I come back." (v. 13). The natural activities of this world are supposed to be continued, not in one's self-interest but in the service of God. This eschatological perspective casts doubt on trust in possessions (which are the result of trade) and so relativizes the importance of trade for a life full of purpose. Thus the Epistle of James warns: "Come now, you who say, 'Today or tomorrow we will go to such and such a town and spend a year there, doing business and making money'. Yet you do not even know what tomorrow will bring." (James 4:13f.). In the *individualized* view of the virtues catalogued in the NT, the "sanctification of life" does not extend only to relations with the family, with husband or wife, but also to professional ethics; e.g. "that no one go beyond and defraud a brother in any matter" (1. Thess. 4:6).

In Revelations, there is a drastic description of the merchants' despair and the futility of the magnificent trade ships as a result of the decline of Babylon (Rev. 18, 9–19).

Summarizing observations

1. Trade, both as domestic trade and long-distance (international) trade, is regarded in the Bible as natural and affirmed as a matter-of-course reality. Long-distance trade was an important motor for growth and prosperity even in the times of the ancient Orient.
2. Then again, the texts reveal the transitoriness of trade relations – flourishing world trade centres always have come and gone – and the various dangers arising from their abuse. The prophets reveal the tightrope walk of trade: it is judged as favourable, but at the same time criticized if it is associated with expectation of salvation. The prophet revealed the limits of global trade
3. In Biblical terms, trade is fair if
   – it is not abused for purposes of power politics (Ezek. 28:6),
   – it does not oppress and exploit anyone (Ezek. 28:16),
   – it deals in goods, but not in people, i.e. slaves (Joel 4:4; Amos 1:9),
   – grants producers a fair wage (Isa. 23:3),
   – admits of redistribution, and of fair and widespread profit participation (Isa. 23:18).
4. The NT texts place trade, like any other activity in life, into the perspective of the kingdom of God and God's justice. This is the yardstick against which trade must be measured.
5. Unjust and unfair trade kills. Just and fair trade enhances life. So direct and simple – despite all the detailed differentiation – are biblical business and trade ethics.

Today

Global economy   Global politics   Global ethics

Vision

Global economy   Global politics   Global ethics

Harmonize development speeds by accelerating globalized politics and ethics while decelerating the globalized economy.

Time lag: The global economy needs global ethics
The very different rates of globalization generate tensions. Economically, globalization is highly developed; politically, far less so; ethically, the evolution of global ethics takes a very long time. However, a globalized economy can only be sustained with globalized politics and ethics and efforts to close the time gap.

Today, one of the main determining factors in trade is globalization. Foreign trade has always crossed borders, but never before has it been so comprehensively global and extensive. Trade ethics must therefore also try to assess globalization in ethical terms; only a rough outline can be provided here.

"World", "globe", "monde", "Welt" – or "oikos"?

These words are backed up by *Weltanschauungen*. The Anglo-Saxon *"globalization"* and the French *"mondialisation"* are secularized terms for that which encompasses the world, which in the Christian view of the world is expressed with the Greek term *"oikos"*: the world as the common house, the House of God. *"oikos"* has three topical dimensions:

- *Economy:* responsible husbandry in production and the fair distribution of material goods.
- *Ecology:* the responsible use, maintenance and renewal of the natural foundations of life.
- *Ecumenism:* the responsible community of people and peoples with different religions and cultures.

This expresses a basically positive attitude towards the overall view of this planet as "One World", provided that this idea is dealt with responsibly.

In ethical terms, globalization has two faces

The definitions of and the literature about globalization are boundless (→ Literature). A provisional ethical assessment of globalization is expressed in the following proposition, which is based on the fundamental values expounded in chapter 3.

Globalization must be our goal if it involves an attempt to understand the world as One Mankind and One Ecosystem together with their interdependence, as long as it envisions fertile ground supporting life in dignity with a fair share for everyone.

Globalization must be rejected if it involves an attempt to reduce the world's multiplicity to one standardized economic, cultural and political model which is created by only a few agents, and in which the economy has priority over any other sphere of life and action.

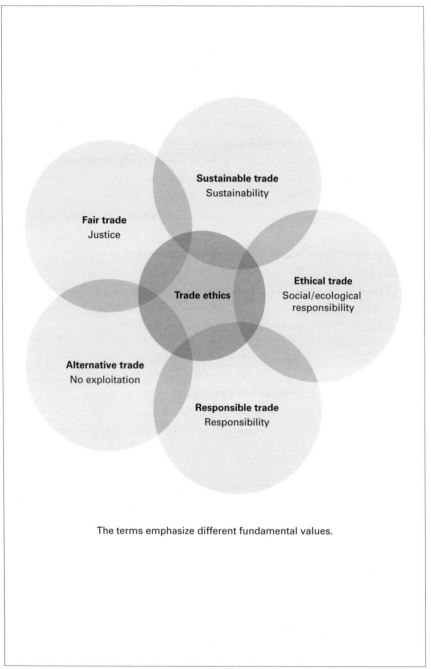

The terms emphasize different fundamental values.

Fundamental terms reflect fundamental values

Ethically sound trade has been given a variety of labels in the last three decades. These labels signal fundamental values and accents with various degrees of emphasis. At the same time, they reveal that in a free-market economy, ethics keeps trying to "market" itself as a "product" which is described as "new" and slightly modified. What fundamental values and accents are behind the terms?

"Alternative trade"

Alternative trade (*commerce alternatif, comercio alternativo*) has been carried on in aid of "third world shops" since the late 1960s, i.e. since the first decade of development; it conceived of itself as a clear rejection of and an alternative to prevalent world trade, which was regarded as exploitative. The first third world shop was set up in the Netherlands in 1969; in 1970, there were already 100 shops there. The idea was to have the recent political decolonialization followed by economic decolonialization and to help producers in developing countries to become independent.

"Fair trade"

Fair trade (*commerce équitable, comercio justo*), which replaced the term "alternative trade" in the mid-1980s, was coined when this trade went beyond the niche shops to include large-scale distributors and commercial trade partners. The epithet "fair" highlights the fundamental value of justice with fair pay and fair prices, as do the adjectives "équitable" in French, "justo" in Spanish and "gerecht" in German. Today, "fair trade" is the most frequently used designation of trade that has particularly ethical characteristics. Many companies lay claim to a small "f"; a capital "F" precisely describes trade as carried out by fair trade organizations (→ chs. 5.11, 6.8).

"Sustainable trade"

Sustainable trade (*commerce durable, comercio sostenible*) takes up the notion of sustainability, which has been used worldwide ever since the 1992 World Conference on Environment and Development in Rio de Janeiro. It focuses on ecology and, as a rule, emphasizes the classic triangle of the economic, ecological and social dimensions of sustainability (IUED, 2001).

"Ethical trade"

Ethical trade (*commerce éthique, comercio ético*) has had less currency to date but is used in certain sectors, such as "ethical investment" or "ethics funds". It describes an overall ethical responsibility in the sense of ethical management systems but tends to emphasize social responsibility (or a combination of ecological and social responsibility). It is frequently employed as an overall term for the above-mentioned element, often with a certain lack of precision.

"Responsible trade"

Responsible trade (*commerce responsable, comercio responsable*) has not yet achieved common currency, but I propose that it is capable of expressing an agent's comprehensive, equivalent ethical responsibility in trade with regard to any stakeholders. The term "responsibility" is more comprehensive than the term "accountability" that is often used in social economies. As far as religion-based ethics is concerned, this also includes the responsibility towards God in response to God's call.

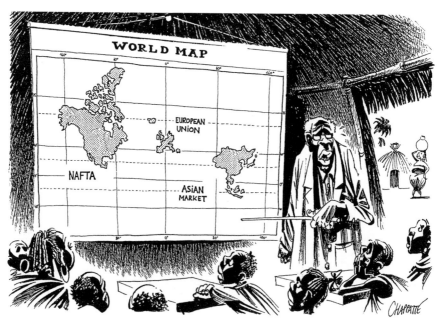

Source: Swiss Coalition News 25/2000

2

Basics II
Methods of ethics

Trade business administration works with methods of product range planning, pricing and profit-oriented controlling. Economics operates with, say, econometric methods, while chemistry uses a wide variety of analytical methods. By the same token, there are methods in ethics which enable us to reach transparent, comprehensible and communicable value judgements, explain the reasoning that is behind them, and produce an analysis of their effects. As in other disciplines, these methods are varied, and they are influenced by pre-scientific premises and value assumptions.

Thus ethics is not simply "a feeling of what is right or wrong", as is often assumed. This feeling is important for our numerous daily decisions, since it is an expression of internalized moral convictions with which we were brought up or which we have worked out and condensed into our own overall view.

The following chapter is meant to provide a few "tools" for ethically responsible decision-making (a detailed history of their origins, and an exposition of the reasons for their use, would be beyond the confines of this book). Thus it shows, for instance, the various levels of ethical commitment, seven methodological steps towards an ethical judgment, types of ethical reasoning, methods of dealing with value conflicts, compromises, ethical processes or factual constraints.

Degrees of the binding character of ethics

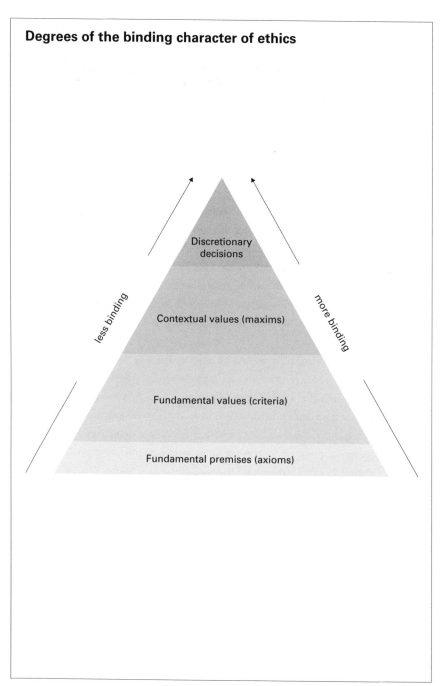

Values and standards

Ethical values describe those ethical foundations from which individual and collective action takes its bearings, and against which it measures its correctness and appropriateness. Values identify that which is valuable and worth achieving. Value ethics (→ ch.1.1) is based on widely applicable fundamental values. Originally, value was an economic term (utility value, exchangeable value, real value, added value).

Ethical standards are often equated with values. The term "standard", however, is less concise and more ambiguous: standards may be a) empirically determined mean values, b) ideas, fundamental values or practical values, c) standardized measuring units (such as the ISO standard), d) legally binding imperatives, or e) aesthetic criteria.

Varying degrees of the binding character of ethics

The *fundamental premise* is the preliminary decision which cannot be substantiated on rational grounds; it is a certainty based on experience and is confessional in nature: "I want to live", "I am loved", "I trust in God".

Fundamental values are basic values/standards which are independent of context and have long-term validity. They are also called *criteria* or *ideal standards*. They are characterized by the fundamental premise but can be understood without it. Freedom and justice are cases in point; they are treated in chapter 3.

Situational and contextual values, also described as *maxims* or *practical standards*, must be distinguished from the fundamental values. Their degree of bindingness is "medium" because they give the fundamental values a concrete shape in relation to individual situations and conditions. One example is Sunday working hours in a certain country in the light of the freedom of trade and social justice. This is explained in chapter 6.

Discretionary decisions have least claim to overall ethical validity. They are decisions where no fundamental ethics values come into play or where the value judgment may go one way or the other for good ethical reasons as, for example, in the choice of the colour for the packaging of a product.

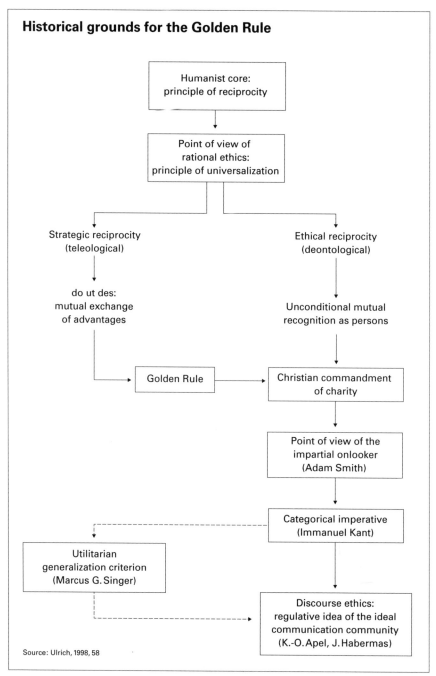

Historical grounds for the Golden Rule

Humanist core:
principle of reciprocity

Point of view of
rational ethics:
principle of universalization

Strategic reciprocity
(teleological)

Ethical reciprocity
(deontological)

do ut des:
mutual exchange
of advantages

Unconditional mutual
recognition as persons

Golden Rule

Christian commandment
of charity

Point of view of the
impartial onlooker
(Adam Smith)

Categorical imperative
(Immanuel Kant)

Utilitarian
generalization criterion
(Marcus G. Singer)

Discourse ethics:
regulative idea of the ideal
communication community
(K.-O. Apel, J. Habermas)

Source: Ulrich, 1998, 58

A) Different grounds for the same value

There are standards which are recognised by all types of *Weltanschauungen* but are substantiated on different grounds. One of these is the *Golden Rule*, which popularly runs: "Don't do to others what you don't want done to yourself." In Jesus's Sermon on the Mount, it is formulated in positive terms: "Therefore all things whatsoever ye would that men should do to you, do ye even so to them" (Matt. 7:12). This Golden Rule can be substantiated in terms of rational ethics, religion or utilitarianism, as the graph on the left shows.

B) Different grounds for different values

The types of ethical argumentation listed below, however, often result in greatly differing, indeed contradictory, values, aims and decisions. Thus the Golden Rule will not be accorded any great importance by the ethics of power whose supreme value is the preservation of (one's own) power.

C) Main types of ethical grounds

These very simplified types overlap in many places.

- *Religion:* Good is whatever God has revealed as good (in different religions through holy scriptures, believers, or nature).
- *Rational ethics:* Good is whatever reason recognises as good; i.e., whatever can be rationally understood on the basis of experience and tradition.
- *Utilitarianism:* Good is whatever produces the greatest benefit for the greatest number of people.
- *Behaviourism:* Good is the behaviour normally displayed by the average human being.
- *Eudaemonism:* Good is whatever increases my happiness.
- *Power ethics:* Good is whatever serves the attainment/preservation of power.
- *Situation ethics:* Good is whatever is appropriate to any individual situation. There are no timeless fundamental values.
- *Conviction ethics:* It is not the objective action that is decisive, but one's inner conviction/motivation/intention.
- *Responsibility ethics:* Good is everything whose consequences are good. Only the real effects and consequences of an action are decisive, not the motivation that has led to them.

Ethical decision-making process

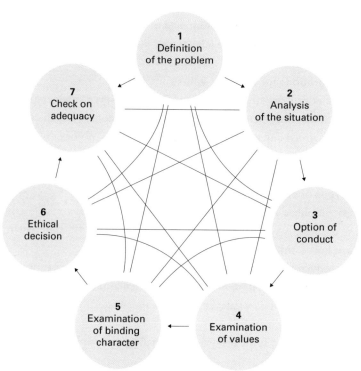

The seven steps show the process whereby standards are substantiated and chosen. This is followed by a process in which the standards are put into force and enforced.

© Stückelberger: Global Trade Ethics

An ethically reflected decision is not simply a feeling, as many would appear to think, but is as clearly structurable in terms of methods as the solution of a logistics or management problem in a company. The seven methodological steps by the theological ethicist, Heinz Eduard Tödt (→ Literature), are widely applied today.

The seven steps towards an ethical decision

1. *Definition of the problem*
   Answer the questions: What is the actual ethical problem? What ethical question do we need to answer? To what extent are our own interests involved? What is the ethical conflict?

2. *Analysis of the situation*
   For what situation(s) must the problem be solved? Conduct an empirical, if possible interdisciplinary examination of the real contexts, their common denominators and differences.

3. *Options of conduct*
   State the possible (and seemingly impossible) options, alternatives and scenarios for action. Formulate possible aims, one of which will have to be chosen, and establish the means that are necessary for their achievement.

4. *Examination of standards*
   On what values is the decision supposed to be based? On what fundamental values, in particular, and on what grounds? On what situational maxims? On what preference rules?

5. *Examination of binding character*
   To what extent do the options of conduct and the values examined imply an ethically and communicatively binding character above and beyond subjective value preference?

6. *Decision*
   Now make the ethically justifiable decision on the basis of the first five steps. In particular, make sure that a connection is established between fundamental values that are independent of the situation, and that the context is taken into account.

7. *Check on adequacy (ethical controlling)*
   When the decision has been made and its consequences are discernible, determine whether the decision was appropriate to the problem, its analysis and the values involved, or whether it must be ethically corrected.

Solving value conflicts

Value conflicts

A, B, C = fundamental values

Solution1: One absolute value

One value prevails over all the others.
No sustainable solution.

Solution 2: Value relations

The values are placed in relation to
each other (relationality)

Solution 3: Preferential rules

If situation X,
then priority of C over B and A

If situation Y,
then priority of P1 over P2 and P3

© Stückelberger: Global Trade Ethics

Value clashes

Both fundamental values and practical values often clash with each other. This reflects differing needs, points of departure, interests, aims and possible courses of action. The clash between ecology and economy is among the most difficult. How can we find an ethically responsible solution to value clashes?

Rendering one fundamental value absolute

This is often done in that one fundamental value is rendered absolute, with the consequence that corresponding countermovements are triggered, which in turn are subject to the danger of a one-value dictatorship. For example, solidarity rendered absolute leads to repressive communism, and freedom rendered absolute leads to untrammelled capitalism.

The relational nature of fundamental values

The relational nature of fundamental values, i.e., the fact that individual fundamental values are inter-related with each other, means that they are not absolute in nature but positioned in relation to other fundamental values or even their opposite values (complementarity). This allows for interrelated ethical action which takes its bearings from value systems. For example, relational freedom leads to freedom in solidarity, and relational solidarity leads to solidarity in freedom.

Preference rules / value judgments

Preference rules attempt to solve a value clash by fixing a set of priorities regarding fundamental or practical values. The basic structure is as follows: in situation X, fundamental value (criterion) C is given preference over fundamental values B and C; in situation Y, fundamental values A and B are both recognised, while practical value (maxim) P1 is given preference over practical values P2 and P3.

For example, there is a value clash between "prosperity for everybody" and "ecological sustainability" in that an increase of foodstuffs production and their worldwide trade/transport may result in ecological damage. Here, a preference rule may stipulate as follows: if the short-term satisfaction of needs may result in the destruction of long-term basic necessities, then the protection of such basic necessities is preferable to the consumption of goods that are not necessary for survival.

Ten compromise guidelines

1. Compromise	→	Possibilism/dynamic	✓
2. Compromise	→	Pragmatism/static	stop
3. Compromise	→	Recognition, fundamental values	✓
4. Compromise	→	Provisional, not definitive	✓
5. Compromise	→	Strengthen the weaker party	✓
6. Compromise	→	Settle conflicts	✓
	→	Cover up conflicts	stop
7. Compromise	→	Quick, to avoid victims	✓
8. Compromise	→	Established in public	✓
9. Compromise	→	Legitimize dictatorships	stop
10. Compromise	→	Destroy basic necessities	stop

© Stückelberger: Global Trade Ethics

Decisions which have to be made by different interest groups almost always involve compromises. Ethically justifiable political, corporate or personal (e.g., consumption-oriented) decisions thus face the question as to whether a compromise is in order, and if so, whether it is ethically acceptable or not.

The definition of compromise

A compromise is a process whereby, voluntarily or under pressure, interests are balanced so as to achieve parts of clashing interests while both parties agree not to achieve their respective aims in full.

Types of compromise

a) *Two areas:*

A *social compromise* entails the balancing of interests between social groups, companies, governments, etc. An *ethical compromise* weighs up values, rules or ethical instances.

b) *Three levels:*

With an *intrapersonal compromise*, a human being attempts to weigh various values internally. *Interpersonal compromises* are made between people, *institutional compromises* between institutions.

c) *Two qualities:*

A tactical or sham compromise does not involve any material decisions; instead, a formula is agreed upon which can be interpreted in different ways. A genuine compromise, however, paves the way for a feasible solution, with both parties relinquishing part of their claims.

d) *Two intensities:*

A *democratic compromise* is a contractual compromise of balanced interests. *Brotherly/friendly compromises* are based on the consensus of communities with similar objectives. However, these are prone to "repressive brotherliness" exercised by authorities of such communities.

e) *Two schedules:*

A distinction can be made between *provisional* and *definitive compromises*.

Justifications for compromises

The justifications for compromises, like the justifications for their rejection, varies a great deal according to the theological or philosophical approach that is used. Compromises may be justified in terms of responsibility ethics, peace ethics, anthropology, the doctrine of creation, Christology or eschatology. This cannot be treated in any more detail here (for more, cf. STÜCKELBERGER 1988, pp. 496–501).

Compromise guidelines

1. A compromise is justified if it constitutes a means towards the end of ethical values and aims. It thus corresponds to possibilism, which always strives for the best possible solution. It is constantly given direction according to ethical aims.
2. A compromise must be rejected if it is seen as a limited value in itself. An ethically acceptable compromise is thus distinct from pragmatism, which refrains from the realization of wide-ranging aims.
3. No compromise is ethically acceptable with regard to the recognition of and basic aspiration to fundamental values (→ ch. 3) and human rights. However, compromises are admissible and necessary when it comes to value judgments and to the social implementation of fundamental values.
4. As a rule, ethically acceptable compromises are provisional compromises made with the intention of replacing them with ethically better compromises at a later date.
5. As a rule, a compromise should be of advantage to the various parties involved. However, it should provide the weaker parties with more advantages than the stronger parties, in support of the fundamental value of commutative justice (→ ch. 3.2).
6. A compromise is good if it helps settle conflicts. It should not be made when it covers up conflicts. The time of the conclusion of a compromise is at its ethical best when, in relative terms, the conflict can be resolved best.
7. Exceptionally, a compromise that works faster but is worse with regard to the attainment of the aims involved must be preferred to a better compromise if this serves to prevent the sacrifice of human or animal life.
8. Because a compromise that has been established in public enjoys a democratic basis, it is usually ethically better than a compromise that has been worked out at the exclusion of the public.

9. The rejection of a compromise may be justified if a compromise which must be regarded as ethically unacceptable (e. g., according to guidelines 3 or 6) would only serve the reinforcement of misanthropic power, such as the legitimation of a dictatorial government through trade agreements.
10. Not all areas of conflict allow for compromise. The rejection of compromise is ethically imperative if a compromise destroys life and basic necessities, or does not lessen the dangers being faced.

Process-oriented ethics

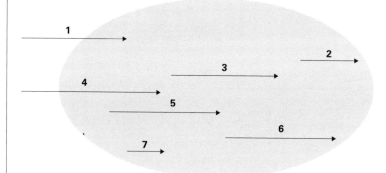

In process-oriented ethics, the direction in which individual or collective conduct develops, and the speed of ethical change, are almost as important as the point of departure and actual practice.

Numbers 1–7 designate various agents with varying points of departure and varying duration of ethically reflected action. The ellipsis indicates the limits of what is defined as ethically acceptable.

Static benchmarks

As a rule, the rating of companies according to ethical criteria ($\rightarrow$ ch. 4.11) measures and assesses a certain conduct and thus the state of a company at a certain point in time. Defined benchmarks are used to measure whether a company satisfies certain financial, ecological, social and societal criteria, or not. Accordingly, a company may be granted a fair-trade or bio label, meet an ISO standard, be given a score from a rating agency for ethical investment, or sign a code of conduct and give evidence of compliance with it ($\rightarrow$ chs. 4.1–4.7).

Process-oriented ethics

This static view is helpful and often necessary for the measurability of ethical conduct. As far as the factual improvement of conduct is concerned however, the direction in which a company, non-governmental organization or government trade institution is moving, is of equal importance. If an agent is moving in the direction of a relatively more ethical type of conduct, this must be rated positively in ethical terms even if he is still lagging behind others. If, say, an industry that has traditionally been damaging to the environment has made efforts and thus contributed to the solution of the problem, those efforts may be even greater than those of a service industry which has few environmental problems and satisfies environmental criteria more easily.

This relational view regards present practice not only in relation to an absolute point of reference but assesses it in relation to the agent's relative point of departure. However, even if the point of departure is unpropitious, the framework of fundamental values ($\rightarrow$ graph on the left) must still be respected totally.

Transition labels

This results in process-oriented labels, such as "transition labels". They characterize companies in transition towards more ethical conduct. More information about labels may be found in chapter 4.5.

Types of structural constraints

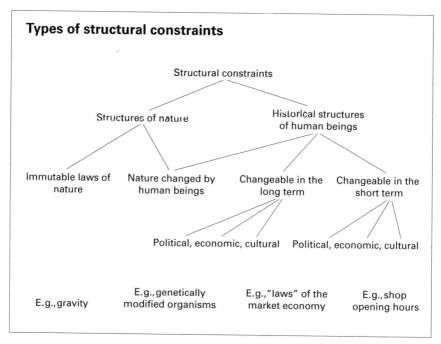

Bandwidth of possible action

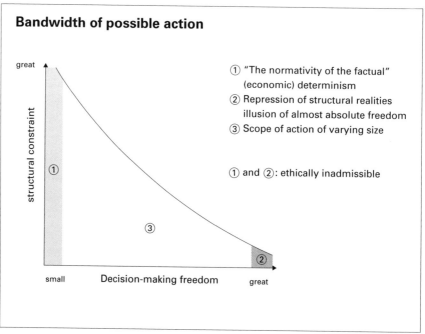

© Stückelberger: Global Trade Ethics

Types of structural constraints ("factual constraints")

So-called factual constraints – an apter name would be structural constraints – consist of two large categories: structures that exist independent of human influence, and structures which have been created by humans and have become historical. Natural laws are unchangeable and cannot be influenced. Owing to an increase in interference with intrinsically natural structures, however, the borderline between nature and culture is becoming increasingly blurred, and thus the proportion of historical structures becomes greater. With regard to these, the long-term or short-term character of changeability is of particular ethical importance to us fast-moving people. In the special legal structures and "constraints", there is a tension between law and ethics, legality and morality.

The bandwidth of possible action

The smaller the structural constraint, the bigger the possibility of immediate action. The bigger the structural constraint, the greater the necessity for the mediate assumption of responsibility through structural change. In this context, two extremes are ethically inadmissible (graph, bottom, areas 1 and 2). What is perceived as unchangeable (factual) must not be elevated into an ethical standard; this "normativity of the factual", these "naturalistic fallacies", negate decision-making options and thus ethics per se. Yet the repression of structural realities is also inadmissible since it precludes any responsible relationship with the structures in question.

Responsible treatment of structural constraints

- Establish what type the structural constraint is (→ graph on the left).
- Indicate the value premises of so-called "factual constraints", e. g. the "partiality of factual constraints" in the market economy (P. ULRICH).
- Consult structural/institutional ethics (→ ch. 1.4) to serve as an ethics for the change of existing structural constraints.
- Determine the temporal dimension of the changeability of structural constraints in order to discover possible courses of action.
- Name the agents that may bring change despite structural constraints. The greater the power, the greater the responsibility.

Aim: to discover the potential for decision-making in order to be able to assume ethical responsibility.

2.8 "For the good that I would, I do not: but the evil which I would not, that I do."

Ethics is concerned not only with great aims and values but also with their practicability. At the same time, one of the most painful basic human experiences is the one that was expressed by Paul: "For the good that I would, I do not: but the evil which I would not, that I do." (Rom. 7:19). This leads us to the contemplation of *human nature*: the question as to the evil and destructive elements in every human being, the desire for the forbidden fruit, the difference between intention and actual action (which is evident in every survey of consumer behaviour), guilt and liberating forgiveness, and the driving forces behind ethical conduct.

Christian ethics is predicated on a realistic view of human nature in that it assumes every human being, no matter how virtuous he or she appears on the outside, to possess an unfathomable destructive potential. However, Christian ethics does not stop there fatalistically but *shows ways out of this trap at the same time*: the insight into and the admission of this incapacity liberates people from know-it-all behaviour, the repression of guilt and the absolutisms and fundamentalisms (economic as well as religious) resulting from this. The *perspective of forgiveness liberates people from the compulsion to claim innocence!* It opens their eyes to realistic steps towards ethical responsibility without people having to defend and justify their conduct as being "no worse than that of others". It also liberates people from individualistic narrowness and leads them towards the *perception of "structural evil"*, i.e., of life-destroying structures such as institutionalized border crossing connected with the compulsion to grow, or in collective addiction behaviour.

(Trade) ethics also looks for *interdisciplinary cooperation* with business psychology, business sociology, business pedagogics, with consumer sociology, environmental psychology, etc. It takes into account the result of motivation research in that, for instance, competence motivation is accorded more weight than deficiency motivation, and in that it emphasizes the affective significance of business-ethical values.

3

Fundamental values

The notion of "value" in ethics and the economy

In *ethics*, *"values"* denote orientation standards and objectives which guide and steer people's actions. They are constitutive for every cultural, social and economic system and thus also for economic action. In the *economy*, *"values"* denote the exchange, utility and capitalized value of goods, and serve as a yardstick for their scarcity. Their value is measured against demand, usefulness and relative rarity. "Value" also denotes the financial earning power of companies (shareholder value). The economic notion of value is older than its ethical counterpart.

Fundamental values are primary values/standards that are independent of any context and possess long-term validity. They are also called criteria or ideal standards (→ ch. 2.1). They are characterized by preliminary decisions referring to experience or *Weltanschauung* (fundamental premises) but can be understood without these. Fundamental values inform, for instance, corporate objectives and guidelines but indirectly also shape day-to-day decisions.

To be distinguished from fundamental values:

Fundamental rights are basic rights guaranteed by a constitution, economic freedom being a case in point. They are formulated in the early part of a constitution; in the Swiss Federal Constitution, they are contained in articles 7–36. Fundamental values are the basis of fundamental rights but are not exhausted in them since ethics transcends what can be fixed in law.

Maxims/practical standards are context-related, concrete expressions of fundamental values. They are not treated in chapter 3 but in the following chapters which deal with ethical standards.

Value-related order principles are basic structures in society as a whole or in its parts, such as constitutionality, the market economy or the WTO's non-discrimination principle.

The tree of fundamental values

(The interdependency of the eleven fundamental values)

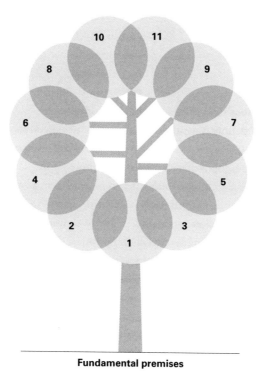

Fundamental premises

Eleven fundamental values

Preservation of life, justice, freedom, sustainability, peace, solidarity, dignity, partnership, trust, power-responsibility, forgiveness.

The eleven fundamental values explained in the following chapter constitute a tree. They overlap in many places. No fundamental value must be rendered absolute; rather, they must all be practised in their relations with each other (relational nature; cf. ch. 2.4). Each branch contains a living part of the whole tree. Accordingly, it does not matter which fundamental value you choose as the starting point for your reading or action. What is of crucial importance is that it will lead you to the other fundamental values. The tree of fundamental values is rooted in experience-related and worldview-related fundamental premises (ch. 2.1).

Value-related institutions are institutions which embody certain fundamental values and implement them institutionally. Examples are political parties, associations, religious communities, government, and marriage/partnerships.

Eleven fundamental values

What fundamental values should provide business ethics, and trade ethics in particular, with a basis? In view of the acceptability and coherence of human action, they must basically be the same that apply to any other spheres of action.

This trade ethics is based on *eleven fundamental values,* which are described below. Their intrinsic substance is of extreme importance. Their grounds have been explained elsewhere (→ Literature); they must be largely omitted in this book (about practical standards, → chs. 4–6).

Roots (fundamental premises) of these fundamental values

General basic human experiences and insights
- I want to live.
- I cannot live/survive on my own, but only in a community.
- All of us humans want to and should live/survive in dignity.
- Other human beings and fellow creatures have a right to life and a will to live which are basically comparable to my own.
- I cannot generate my own life. It is given, a gift.
- The world as a creation is beautiful and rich in diversity.
- The discovery of foreign things is an enrichment but also creates fear.
- I make mistakes and need an opportunity to restart again and again.

Specifically Christian basic and religious experiences
- God as the magnificent Creator wants life in its diversity. Our astonishment at and gratitude for this creation are the foundation of responsible action.
- God as Jesus Christ wants to save life, not destroy it.
- God as a liberating spiritual force is basically able to work in all human beings. All human beings receive their inalienable dignity and their rights from God.
- God is communication. For a successful life, human beings need communication and community, and also a religious community which includes communion with people of different religious convictions.
- Community and peace require a fair distribution of goods and rights.
- Human decision-making freedom is an expression of the love of God. This also includes the freedom to carry out destructive acts. Forgiveness vanquishes despair.
- God adheres to the covenant with humankind, indeed with God's entire creation, despite repeated failure, and always enables us to start again.
- Life on earth is not everything, "only" the great foretaste of greater, eternal abundance. The serenity arising from this assurance liberates us from gread.

Dimensions of poverty

Lack of material
resources

Short life

Illiteracy

Exclusion

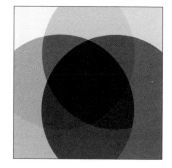

The dimension may overlap in
different ways.

Dimensions of the preservation of life

Vital resources:
food
clothing
housing

Health

Education
Access to
information

Relationships
Security

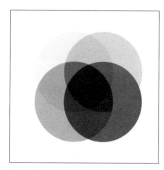

The dimension may overlap in
different ways.

Source: UNDP 1997/Author's own layout

© Stückelberger: Global Trade Ethics

The simple preservation of life is indeed a great aim, considering that some 800 million people still suffer from hunger, millions of small children die, and people are killed in wars. The fundamental value *preservation of life* means the creation of the material, psychological and intellectual conditions for human and non-human life to be able to evolve in their basic functions. The preservation of life is the prerequisite for the realization of life as aspired to in fundamental values such as freedom, justice and participation.

The fight against poverty: an economic aim

The fundamental value *preservation of life* implies a poverty-oriented development and economic strategy, such as has been pursued by the UN Development Programme (UNDP) for some time, and by the World Bank since the late 1990s. The causes of poverty include not only a lack of food, clothing and housing, but also a lack of education, health and social integration (→ graph on the left).

Basic-need-oriented welfare economics

For business ethics, the fundamental value *preservation of life* also means economic activity that takes its bearings from basic needs. An "economics of more and more for fewer and fewer people" is replaced by an "economics of enough for all" (the expressions were coined by GOUDZWAARD/DE LANGE, 1990). According to the strategies for the fight against poverty, basic needs include not only all the material necessities of life, but also education combined with access to means of communication for people to be able to provide themselves with information, and a network of relationships which in turn provides security.

Welfare economics – from Adam SMITH's *Wealth of Nations* (1776) to Arthur PIGOU's *The Economics of Welfare* (1920) and Vilfredo PARETOS *New Welfare Economics* (1927) – looks for an optimal increase in economic welfare. It does not, however, solve the important problem of *justice with regard to distribution* and the *"option for the poor"* (→ ch. 3.2). In any case, trade in goods and services plays a central part in the implementation of the fundamental value *preservation of life*.

© Stückelberger: Global Trade Ethics

Fairness in trade means fair conditions of exchange. This is a cornerstone of the economy in general and of trade in particular. In a future-oriented business ethics, the fundamental value of justice pertains to the following ten aspects:

1. *Performance-related justice:* justice with regard to performance means that every person (indeed every living being, wether human or not) who is involved in the production, trade, sale or disposal of a product must be given their due on the basis of their performance.

   Justice with regard to performance allows for a fair assessment of and compensation for performance. In trade, this is reflected in a fair exchange in the purchase and sale of products, with the entire production chain from the raw materials down to the end-user and the disposal process being taken into account.

2. *Needs-related justice:* justice with regard to needs means that a fair exchange of goods must take into consideration human need, i.e., the subsistence minimum and a dignified life.

   Apart from performance, human need is the second criterion for economic justice. The fact that human beings are more than their performance and do not acquire their salvation through performance is at the core of the Christian view of humankind. Justice with regard to performance and justice with regard to needs are not opposites but must complement each other because the dignity of human beings and their non-human environment is respected best when both efficiency and its limits and people's dependence on the performance of others is recognized as a criterion for a humane life.

3. *Distributive justice:* justice with regard to distribution ensures that goods are distributed fairly, while performance and needs are taken into measured consideration to pursue the aim of social equalization.

   The shares of countries and continents in world trade are far apart and are growing even further apart; this distribution is an urgent problem of justice. The ethical acceptability of market mechanisms and government and multilateral liberalization or regulation policies must be measured against, among other things, whether they facilitate or inhibit fair distribution.

4. *Justice as equal treatment (among other things, with respect to gender):* this allows for equality of opportunity.

   Equality is a central characteristic of justice throughout the various ethical conceptions of justice. The equality of all human beings is substantiated differently in the different ethical approaches. For theological ethics, equality in terms of the precept of equal treatment is substantiated in various ways: in the theology of creation, by the proposition that all human beings are a living image of God;

47

in Christology (in terms of Christ), in Jesus Christ's offer of liberation, which is addressed to everyone; and in pneumatology, by the spirit of love through which we respect our neighbours as ourselves. The principle of equal treatment and equality of opportunity is also of particular significance in terms of the equal treatment of genders.

5. *Participatory justice:* justice with regard to participation means the fair, appropriate participation in decision-making of all those involved in an economic process.

   Justice is not an absolute quality but must be jointly renegotiated and developed according to the above-mentioned criteria for every new context. Justice is a participative process. This participative structuring of the world economy concerns all the levels from the small producer negotiating a fair price, to democratic participation in the establishment of national trade policies, and to equal rights in government cooperation for the negotiation of international treaties. Fair participation is an essential instrument capable of reducing the number of trade conflicts.

6. *Ecological justice:* justice with regard to ecology means a sustainable use and fair distribution of resources, as well as a reduction in and a fair distribution of ecological burdens. A fair distribution of resources and burdens extends to three dimensions: between generations living today, between today's and tomorrow's generations, and between human beings and their non-human environment.

   When distribution conflicts arise, justice with regard to ecology stipulates the preference rule that the elementary needs (basic needs) of today's or future generations or the non-human environment have priority over the non-elementary needs of today's or future generations or the non-human environment. The right to a subsistence minimum ($\rightarrow$ ch.3.1) has priority over the right to self-realization ($\rightarrow$ ch.3.3). One of the prerequisites for ecological justice is the cost transparency in relation to goods. Ecological justice also contains an eminently peace-securing dimension since the fight for resources is one of the most frequent causes of conflict ($\rightarrow$ ch.6.21). Trade is ethically acceptable when it does justice to the environment and does not appropriate any access to and use of scarce resources by violent means.

7. *Allocation-related justice:* in terms of business ethics, justice with regard to allocation means the fair placement and weighting of production factors, with the other nine aspects of justice taken into due account.

   Allocation – i.e., the allocation of the production factors land/natural resources, labour and capital both in weighting and in geographical allocation – is one of the economy's major tasks. Trade, the worldwide movement of production factors, plays a central role in this. The relation between the global and local dimensions is a problem of this aspect of justice. Trade is fair when allocation is fair. In a market economy, allocation is primarily carried out through pricing. This is why in market-economic conditions, fair prices are crucial for allocation to be fair.

8. *Relational justice:* justice with regard to relationships views a trading partner not merely as an economic object and a homo œconomicus who creates maximum benefits, but also as a human being with whom a relationship is developed.

   The globalized economy results not only in a rapidly increasing mobility of goods, but also of people and of relations between trading partners. "Loyalty" to a producer, or of consumers to a brand or firm, is rapidly decreasing. This aspect of justice raises the question as to how this mobility of relationships, which in many trading sectors is almost total by now, can be replaced by a humane mixture of long-term and changing trade relations without keeping flagging production structures artificially alive. A humane economy always measures economic aims against the wellbeing of people, and thus also of trading partners and their personnel.

9. *Procedural justice:* justice with regard to procedures means calculable, constitutional (publicly and privately) regulated, transparent, corruption-free and thus fair procedures in trade relations.

   Justice with regard to procedures is a necessary constituent, particularly of justice in terms of equal treatment and impartiality, but also in relation to justice with regard to performance, participation and distribution. In trade relations, monitoring, the continuous surveillance of and checks on compliance with trade criteria, is a necessary component of fair procedures.

10. *Interlinked justice* places the various aspects of justice in relation to one another as in a network since no aspect alone is tantamount to justice as a whole. This interlinkage also prevents justice from being rendered absolute. It safeguards the relations (relational nature) with and the equilibrium between the other fundamental values.

    Every fundamental value can become a negative value if it is rendered absolute. The basic ethical value of love unfolds in various fundamental values such as reconciliation, freedom, justice, human dignity, solidarity, etc., which, however, only lead to love if they remain related to one another, relational, interlinked. This is particularly true for the balance between freedom and justice.

1 Personal freedom
3 Ecological freedom
5 Social freedom
7 Freedom of the weaker person
9 Freedom for solidarity
10 Interlinked freedom
8 Freedom for commitments
6 Democratic freedom
4 Ideological freedom
2 Economic freedom

3

© Stückelberger: Global Trade Ethics

Freedom is the prerequisite of ethical action. It is only with freedom of choice that responsibility can be assumed (→ Power/responsibility, ch. 3.10). Everyone wants freedom, but everyone means something different by it. This trade ethics is based on the following understanding of freedom:

Free from ... constraints

Freedom *from* something is central to the general understanding of the term, particularly freedom from restrictions such as are caused by government regulations or interhuman standards and limits. In ethical terms, this also extends to the acquisition of freedom from so-called factual constraints (→ ch. 2.7), from the compulsion of growth, from greed, generally from any life-destroying action.

Free for ... solidarity

The freedom *from* something must lead towards a freedom for something. Only those who are free not only from destructiveness but also free to do good will be able to act ethically. This involves being free for love and solidarity towards other people and creation as a whole, free for commitments and community, and thus for the recognition of social systems and legal systems which not only protect one's own freedom but also the freedom of others. In this context, the measurement of freedom is love and community. Freedom and the obligation to serve the common good are two sides of one and the same coin.

The Protestant churches of Europe jointly described the Christian conception of freedom as follows: "Freedom is not merely compatible with 'love', it is love. Freedom grows in the community, particularly in a community with the victims who remind us of our responsibility. It is in the efforts to attain harmony with creation that freedom will grow."

Ten dimensions of freedom

1. *Personal freedom* means physical and mental wholeness, the free movement of persons and the free choice of allocation, the possession of material and immaterial goods to preserve life.

2. *Economic freedom* means the scope of action in production, trade, sales and the disposal of goods, ideas and services, and the free choice of an economic system.

3. *Ecological freedom* means being free from emissions, damage, inestimable ecological risks, and from the fear of the destruction of the foundations of life.

4. *Ideological freedom* means religious freedom and freedom of conscience, freedom of speech and information, and the free choice of language and culture.

5. *Social freedom* means freedom of assembly and association, the freedom to form a coalition, and the freedom of expression.

6. *Democratic freedom* means the possibility of participating in political and social decision-making processes.

7. *Freedom of the weaker person* means safe havens against the abuse of freedom by stronger persons.

8. *Freedom for commitments* means the will and ability to depend on others in the service of a greater common whole and to avoid isolation and autarchy. Trade, in particular, fundamentally thrives on exchange and relationships.

9. *Freedom for solidarity* means being free from a one-sided pursuit of mere self-interest, and being free for other people's freedom as a prerequisite of community.

10. *Interlinked freedom* considers the various aspects of freedom to be interlinked as in a network, since no one can be free on his or her own. Interlinked freedom is also concerned with the connection and equilibrium with the other fundamental values.

3.4 Sustainability

The definition of sustainability

Sustainable development enables the present generation to live a life in dignity without endangering the life in dignity of future generations or the non-human environment.

This definition of sustainability derives from that expressed in the Brundtland Report which also provided the basis for the 1992 UNCED Conference in Rio de Janeiro: "Sustainable development is development that meets the needs of the present without compromising the ability of future generations to meet their own needs." However, the above definition has been extended by two essential elements. First, the notion of "needs" is backed by the very important basic needs strategy of the Brundtland Report. "Life in dignity", however, transcends the satisfaction of basic (material) needs. Also, "life in dignity" is a value that allows for greatly differing cultural interpretations. Second, my own definition includes not only future generations, but nature, and does so explicitly, not merely implicitly. The non-human environment, too, possesses a dignity that is independent of man.

The five dimensions of sustainability

- The *economic* dimension of sustainable development covers the production and (fair) distribution of goods and services for an existence in dignity for present and future generations and for nature.
- The *ecological* dimension of sustainable development covers the preservation of the basic necessities, resources and eco-systems for an existence in dignity for present and future generations and for nature.
- The *social* and *political* dimension of sustainable development covers the fair equalization of interests through everyone's participation in all the vital decisions for an existence in dignity for present and future generations and for nature, and social peace in particular.
- The *cultural* dimension of sustainable development covers the function of culture as the generator of identity and community for an existence in dignity for present and future generations and for nature.
- The *religious* dimension of sustainable development covers the function of religion as a generator of identity, community and meaning for an existence in dignity for present and future generations and for nature.

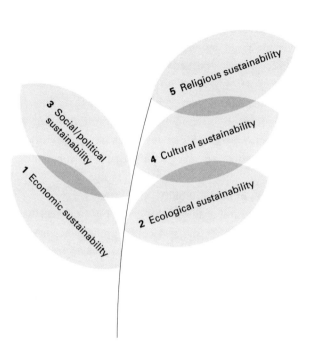

Sustainable development indivisibly contains
ecological, economic and social dimensions.
To this extent, there is extensive international
agreement (in theory; not in practice). The cultural and religious dimensions of sustainability
have so far been rather neglected and must
be taken into more careful consideration, also
with regard to trade.

© Stückelberger: Global Trade Ethics

The interdependency of the five dimensions

No biodiversity without cultural diversity. No economic sustainability without a respect for religious diversity. No social and political sustainability without cultural and religious sustainability.

The five dimensions of sustainability are indivisibly interconnected; this fact has consequences for sustainable trade. Development cannot be sustainable if one of the dimensions is missing or is not placed in relation to the others.

One example may suffice: conflicts about the extraction of raw materials in the living space of indigenous peoples, or growing religious fundamentalisms resulting from a disregard of the religious dimension of globalization strategies and trading activities are signals that sustainability must fail unless it includes cultural and religious understandings and makes efforts to achieve careful and slow transformation based on interfaith dialogue. The serious religious conflicts in Indonesia, a country that was previously a model of religious coexistence, give evidence of the economic setbacks that may be produced. For this reason, there can be no economic sustainability without religious sustainability through respect for religious diversity. Any promotion of trade by means of one-sided economic modernization strategies fails again and again or suffers severe setbacks if the religious roots of values in the society concerned are not taken into account.

The social dimension of sustainability is also concerned with social peace in particular. Economic and ecological sustainability is impossible without social peace, which points towards the next fundamental value, peace. This dimension must be more strongly developed in the concepts of sustainability. The physicist and philosopher, C. F. von WEIZSÄCKER, expressed it pithily: "No peace among people without peace with nature. No peace with nature without peace among people."

7 Peace with nature

8 Reconciliation

5 Social equality

6 Security

3 Fair economic competition

4 Sharing natural resources

1 Absence of military warfare

2 Non-violent conflict resolution

5

© Stückelberger: Global Trade Ethics

Just as the fundamental values of freedom and justice are basically undisputed, so is peace: everyone wants peace, but everyone understands something different by it. Far more than the terms *peace, paix, Friede*, the Judaeo-Christian notion of shalom is more comprehensively expressive of a holistic view.

The basic value of peace with its eight dimensions

1. *Peace as the absence of military warfare* means the absence, between or inside nations, of conflicts which are armed and involve physical violence.
2. *Peace as non-violent conflict resolution* means the ability to settle conflicts without violence from a local level (no small arms) to the global level. Peace does not mean that there are no conflicts.
3. *Peace as fair economic competition* means the rejection of life-destructive economic and trade wars; it means economic activity based on equal opportunity.
4. *Peace as the just distribution of natural resources* means the renunciation of the violent appropriation and defence of basic necessities. Peace contractually regulates the fair distribution of their use.
5. *Peace as social equality* means social partnership with a fair distribution of interests between economic interest groups (stakeholders).
6. *Peace as security* means a network of economic, political, cultural and religious community relations, as well as their constitutionally guaranteed protection.
7. *Peace with nature* means respect for the dignity of non-human entities that is independent of humanity.
8. *Peace as reconciliation* means the transformation of injustice into a new start which may even include loving one's enemy.

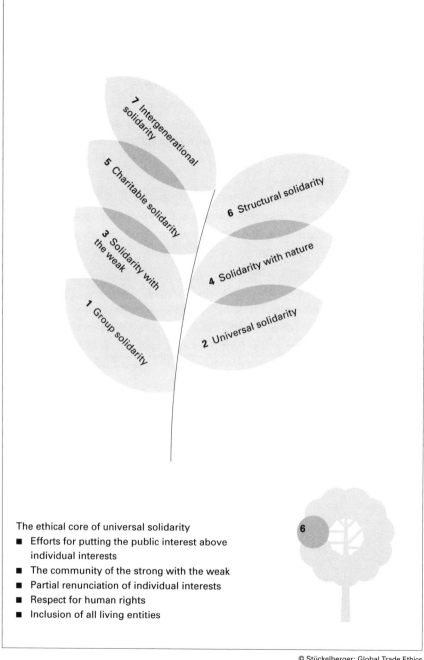

The ethical core of universal solidarity
- Efforts for putting the public interest above individual interests
- The community of the strong with the weak
- Partial renunciation of individual interests
- Respect for human rights
- Inclusion of all living entities

© Stückelberger: Global Trade Ethics

Forms of solidarity: who with whom?

- *Solidarity with peers (group solidarity)* serves the representation of the interests of like-minded people and the reinforcement of one's own group (class, race, nation, gender, profession, generation, industry, religion, etc.). It often runs counter to universal solidarity but can also be its preliminary stage.

- *Solidarity with everyone (universal solidarity)* seeks the integration of and reconciliation with all human beings in the service of (ecological) survival, peace, and loving one's enemy. It is tantamount to a mature, universal ethos. However, it is also capable of concealing conflicts of interest and power structures.

- *Solidarity of the strong with the weak and with nature* allows for the empowerment of helpless and powerless people and also for the protection of non-human entities. It involves a voluntary renunciation of positions of precedence. It may be paternalistic.

- *Solidarity with future generations (intergenerational solidarity)* places particular emphasis on ecological responsibility and sustainability, if necessary at the expense of solidarity with present-day interest groups. It may clash with solidarity with people who are suffering today.

- *Charitable individual solidarity* takes the immediate suffering of individuals seriously but often overlooks its structural causes.

- *Legal/structural solidarity* wants rights instead of alms; it seeks equal opportunities and permanence. Is apt to overlook individuals.

Motives for solidarity: why?

- *Decreed solidarity* is demanded by law, for instance through taxation, community service, and social security contributions.

- *Voluntary solidarity* derives from ideological convictions or personal involvement, but has more arbitrary/selective effects.

- *Democratically agreed solidarity* requires a majority's voluntary conviction and is then transformed into decreed solidarity.

- *Tactical solidarity* merely aims at temporary relationships with others for the attainment of one's own interests.

3.7 **Dignity**

"In the realm of ends, everything has either a price or a dignity. That which has a price can be replaced by something else, as an equivalent; that which is priceless, and thus allows of no equivalent, has a dignity."
Immanuel Kant

Inalienable dignity

Dignity is the intrinsic value of living beings which they are entitled to regardless of their physical, psychical, personal and social characteristics, abilities or deficiencies. Dignity is inalienable (sacrosanct, indisposable) and irreplaceable. No one and nothing can dispossess living beings of their dignity; however, dignity can be violated.

Human dignity and the dignity of creatures

Every human being is entitled to dignity in terms of inalienable human dignity, which is the basis of human rights and the equal nature of all human beings, and is thus a fundamental value and a fundamental notion of modern law (Swiss Federal Constitution, art. 7: "Human dignity shall be respected and protected."). However, there is also an inalienable "dignity of creatures", of the non-human environment. In the Swiss Federal Constitution, this has even become constitutionally protected: "taking into account the dignity of creatures" (art. 120/2), along with security and biodiversity, is a criterion for, say, the assessment of gene-technological interference with living beings. Human dignity and the dignity of creatures are both separate and inseparable; i.e., a distinction must be made between them, but they cannot be divided.

Substantiation and significance of dignity

Dignity is substantiated in different ways, depending on different ideological backgrounds. Theological ethics substantiates it on the grounds of humans being made in the image of God, an image which was not destroyed by the fall, i.e. our guilt-stricken nature, but also in the dual command of love (Love God and your neighbour as yourself) and the Golden Rule (Don't do to others what you don't want done to yourself). The dignity of creatures has its roots in covenant theology, i.e. in God's covenant (with Noah), which was not only concluded with present and future generations but "with every living creature that is with you" (Gen. 9:9–11).

The topical nature of the protection of dignity in terms of business ethics is chiefly found in the domains of labour (dignified working conditions), culture, gender, religion and technological research.

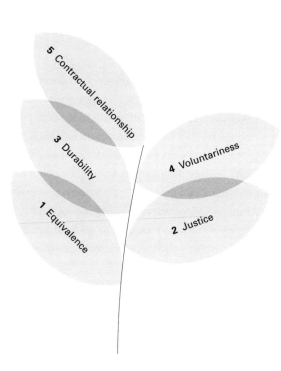

Forms of partnership (in the economy):

- immediate in terms of personal ethics:
  between personnel
- mediate in terms of structural ethics:
  between trading partners
- mediate in terms of structural ethics:
  in economic policy
- immediate in terms of environmental ethics:
  between people and animals
- mediate in terms of environmental ethics:
  in environmental policy

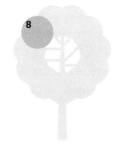

© Stückelberger: Global Trade Ethics

Partnership – also with trading partners

Partnership particularly denotes a direct, long-term relationship between two persons which is based on love (marriage or quasi-marital relationship). There are, however, various other forms of partnership which are based on relationships that are less close: trading and business partners, political and ideological partners, and partnerships between institutions, such as municipal partnerships, development partnerships between countries, partnership between political parties. In a limited way, we may also speak of a partnership between human beings and nature.

Features of ethically responsible partnership

The basic characteristic of partnership is a mutual (reciprocal) relationship between persons or institutions who or which acknowledge each other as responsible human beings. Partnership is predicated on the partners' basic equality, and on their readiness to depend on each other and to have a mutual give-and-take relationship.

In recognition of the other fundamental values on which this trade ethics is based, the following further features characterize a partnership, and also a trading partnership:

1. the partners take each other seriously as responsible subjects;
2. their commitment is voluntary;
3. their relationship aspires to equality and justice;
4. their relationship has been established for a certain duration;
5. their relationship is contractually regulated, calculable and transparent.

Symmetrical and asymmetrical partnerships

The ideal type of partnership is thus a symmetrical relationship. In reality, however, it is usually asymmetrical, for instance with regard to decision-making power and control of resources. Often, partnership is a term of ideological embellishment. This is the case when one partner is completely dependent on the other, so that there is no reciprocity, and a great disequilibrium of power is covered up (for instance, if the relationship between a strong industrialized nation and a developing country is described as a partnership). In such cases, the term partnership ought to be avoided.

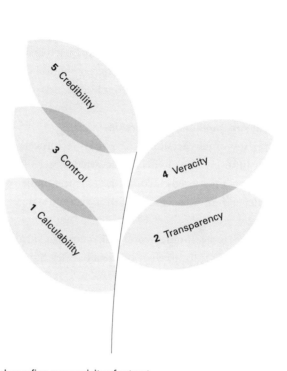

This graph shows five prerequisites for trust.
Types of trust:
1. Unearned trust:
   based on positive expectations
2. Earned trust:
   based on experience
3. Sympathetic trust:
   immediate emotional access
4. Loving trust:
   emotional and cognitive relationships
5. Competence trust:
   based on assessment of competence
6. Environmental trust:
   trust in a person's/institution's environment
7. Delegated trust:
   based on third-party assessment (ratings)

Trust: prerequisite for relationships

Trust is a basic condition of interpersonal relationships, but also of business relationships and in a particularly high degree of trading relationships. Where there is mistrust instead of trust, there is a great risk of sustaining losses or disadvantages through a (trade) relationship. In contract law, the significance of trust is expressed by the fact that "good faith" is a basic category in the domain of contracts and obligations, and is of central importance in trade.

Calculability, transparency and control…

For trust to be able to emerge and grow, three prerequisites are necessary: calculability, transparency and checks.

Calculability, reliability and dependability as the opposite of arbitrariness and as an aspect of loyalty create security, a basis for planning, sustainability and thus trust.

Transparency as *truthfulness*, honesty and openness in a company's information, social and environmental reporting is closely connected with calculability. Embellishment, appeasement, corruption, etc., are contrary to transparent business.

Control is not an opposite of trust, as is popularly suggested. It is not a case of "trust instead of control", but of trust thanks to control, since trust in someone is not something we have or don't have, but something that grows gradually like love and partnership and can be deliberately encouraged. Transparency allows for control that fosters trust and is comprehensible.

…result in credibility

Together with the implementation of the other fundamental values (such as the responsible use of power, and the commitment to sustainability and justice), calculability, transparency and control provide an overall picture that is perceived as credibility. In terms of business ethics, credibility is the most important feature of a company, since it creates trust. To "give someone credit" (in financial terms) also means that you trust that person, and this also pays off in the form of creditworthiness. "Credibility becomes the criterion for the assessment of business-ethical action", THOMMEN concludes in his book on business administration (THOMMEN 1996).

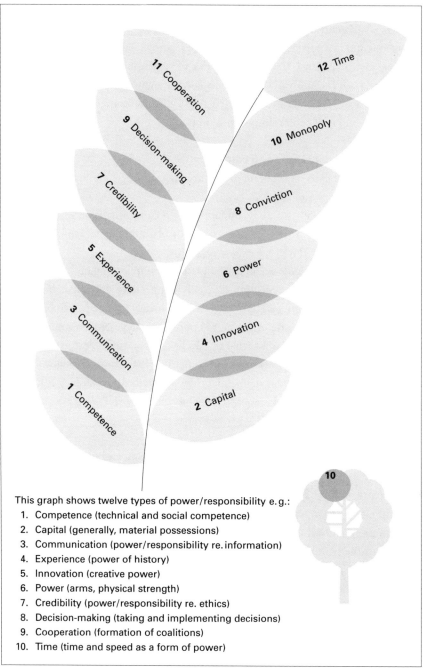

This graph shows twelve types of power/responsibility e.g.:

1. Competence (technical and social competence)
2. Capital (generally, material possessions)
3. Communication (power/responsibility re. information)
4. Experience (power of history)
5. Innovation (creative power)
6. Power (arms, physical strength)
7. Credibility (power/responsibility re. ethics)
8. Decision-making (taking and implementing decisions)
9. Cooperation (formation of coalitions)
10. Time (time and speed as a form of power)

Power and responsibility: inextricably linked

Owing to the fact that power is often abused, power is a pejorative term for many. Can power be a fundamental value? According to Max Weber, power is the capacity to enforce one's own will. As a capacity for the realization and implementation of ethical values, power is positive; indeed, it is necessary. According to the theological definition of the World Council of Churches, power represents humanity's ability to participate in God's creation. This is not a question of having as much power as possible, but of the power that is appropriate to the task and goal at every level of action. Ethically speaking, power and responsibility are inextricably two sides of the same coin, of the same fundamental value. If you have no power, you cannot assume any responsibility, and if you exercise power without any responsibility, you will have to be divested of it because in such a case, the other fundamental values are in jeopardy.

Share and control of power/responsibility

Power and responsibility must be fairly distributed and democratically limited and controlled lest they be abused. Power is a loan for use in the service of a community. The measure of responsibility must be commensurate with the measure of power invested in a person or institution, and vice versa. Responsibility that is not shared will make people feel responsible for things they are perfectly unable to influence, and this is almost as destructive as undivided power. Conversely, it is irresponsible to demand responsibility from others without granting them the corresponding authority.

Power/responsibility towards whom?

In its etymology and semantics, responsibility is linked with the word response; i.e., providing an answer. In rational ethics, this is the responsibility towards reason; in theological ethics, towards God; in discourse ethics, towards the community; in general terms, towards anyone affected by any given action. In the history of thought, responsibility is a further development of the notion of conscience in the wake of the modern emphasis on the individual. Power is tamed by responsibility, reinvested in an authority that is above the holder of power, and thus placed at the service of humanity.

"Merciless competition"

In the fierce global fight for markets, a notion that keeps cropping up is that of *"merciless competition"*. Even the smallest strategic weakness will threaten a company with collapse or a hostile takeover. "The market will give no quarter," is what is said in such situations. Necessary structural change is not supposed to be prevented by false supporting measures. And yet: for an ethically responsible conduct of business according to the fundamental values described, a "merciful economy" should be aspired to. What does this mean?

The "economy of forgiveness": new starts

People and institutions get into seemingly hopeless situations in which normal problem-solution instruments lose their grip. Extraordinary situations require extraordinary solutions; in personal terms, condonation and forgiveness; in politics, measures such as amnesties; in business, bankruptcy proceedings, debt remission, reparation payments, a word of forgiveness. In Christian theological ethics, forgiveness is based on the mercy of God: always offer a new beginning with people who do evil although they want to do good ($\rightarrow$ ch. 2.8). Forgiveness is an act of liberation for a new start, freed from the compulsion to claim to be innocent. Weak, dishonest people are useful, and God chooses them as partners again and again. To forgive does not mean to forget. Guilt is identified and acknowledged. The warning issued by the great Swiss pedagogue, Heinrich Pestalozzi, must be heeded: "justice must not be drowned in the sewer of mercy". Forgiveness is the heart and driving force of comprehensive, new justice ($\rightarrow$ ch. 3.2). Thus a politics and an economy of forgiveness ought to be developed.

"Merciful economy": acceptance of mistakes

The acceptance of mistakes is a modern secular term for this fundamental value. It has emerged particularly as an ethical criterion in the assessment of high-risk new (large-scale) technologies such as nuclear or genetic technology, and stipulates that a technology must ensure that the deficiency of human behaviour which is to be expected not to have any disastrous consequences. The market, too, needs mechanisms for the acceptance of mistakes as a corrective to mercilessness.

4

Instruments of ethical responsibility in trade

After the explanation of the fundamental values which represent the basis of ethically responsible economic activity, the fourth part of the book will now deal with the means and instruments for the promotion of these values. According to the objective of this book, and in the framework of today's globalized market economy, the focal point will be on private possibilities of action on the part of companies and institutions of civil society. In the Anglo-Saxon world, "corporate citizenship" denotes a company's or institution's strategic orientation towards competence, the long-term safeguard of its reputation, ethical standards, and the mutually responsible relationship between itself and society in a global perspective. Of course, national and international government trade policies play a central part in terms of ethically responsible economic action, and are mentioned here, but are not our main concern.

Today, the market is characterized by a wide variety of ethical standards, labels, codes of conduct and declarations which are designed to encourage ethical economic action on a voluntary basis. As gratifying as the spread and increase of these instruments may be, it still results in three ethical challenges: a) It is an indication of the lack of ethics felt by many in our breathtakingly globalized and deregulated economy. The speed of the development of information technology and the economy must be adjusted to the speed of the development of ethics ($\rightarrow$ ch. 6.3). b) The removal of government regulations can only be partially compensated by private ethical standards. It can and must complement the trade-ethical responsibility of the international community yet is incapable of simply replacing it. c) The great diversity of supply must be carefully reviewed in ethical terms and checked for its seriousness. As is well known, ethics in the marketplace has long been a market for ethics, too ($\rightarrow$ ch. 6.24), with products of greatly varying quality.

Planning system for trade companies

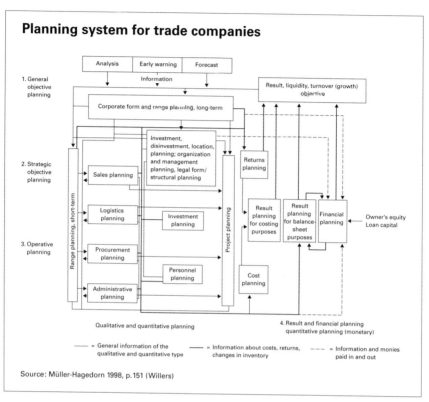

Qualitative and quantitative planning

4. Result and financial planning
quantitative planning (monetary)

───── = General information of the
qualitative and quantitative type

───── = Information about costs, returns,
changes in inventory

─ ─ ─ = Information and monies
paid in and out

Source: Müller-Hagedorn 1998, p.151 (Willers)

Categories of objectives for a company

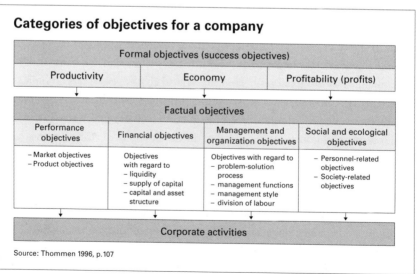

Formal objectives (success objectives)		
Productivity	Economy	Profitability (profits)

Factual objectives			
Performance objectives	Financial objectives	Management and organization objectives	Social and ecological objectives
– Market objectives – Product objectives	Objectives with regard to – liquidity – supply of capital – capital and asset structure	Objectives with regard to – problem-solution process – management functions – management style – division of labour	– Personnel-related objectives – Society-related objectives

Corporate activities

Source: Thommen 1996, p.107

Ethics in all areas of planning

A serious and long-term trade ethics seeks to involve all the levels and steps of corporate planning, as they are represented in the upper graph on the left (→ also chs. 1.4 and 1.5). This begins in the selection of questions to be analyzed. The focus then homes in on growth and result objectives (→ ch. 6.7 on profit), and on product range, logistics, procurement and investment planning.

Ethically reviewed corporate objectives

It is rewarding for an ethically responsible company to measure and review the various success and factual objectives represented in the lower graph on the left against the eleven fundamental values described in chapter 3. In this context, social, ecological and development-political objectives should not merely be located in areas related to personnel and society, but also in the core areas, i.e. in what should be produced, bought and sold where, by whom, at what price, and within what period of time.

Planning instruments

- Ethical questions and inputs (e.g., from signed corporate codes of conduct) in the planning parameters provided by management.
- Ethical training of personnel responsible for planning and of other personnel.
- Ethical coaching of management.
- Involvement of value-related aspects in the discourse with shareholders at AGMs.
- Involvement of the personnel's ethical and religious attitude in interviews, and support of their ethical and religious roots outside working hours.
- Corporate strategy for the introduction of labels, signature of codes of conduct, etc. (→ chs. 4.4 – 4.6).

This incorporation of business ethics in "normal" planning processes corresponds to a company's long-term, sustainable "credibility strategy" (J.-P. THOMMEN).

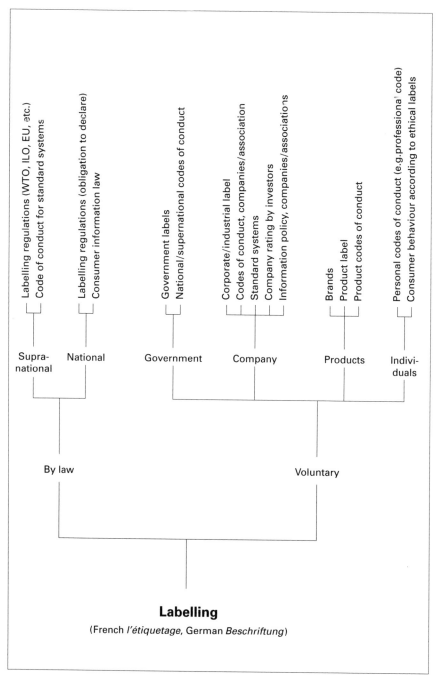

Labelling

(French *l'étiquetage*, German *Beschriftung*)

Public and private product labelling

Product labelling (synonymous with French *étiquetage* and German *Beschriftung*) is the umbrella term for an important trade instrument which identifies product characteristics such as the nature, quality, origin and manner of production in words and/or a symbol, thus making products comparable and distinguishable.

On the one hand, this labelling is carried out nationally, regionally or internationally in accordance with compulsory government provisions (EU, WTO). On the other hand, it is done with a wide variety of voluntary private systems, such as brands, labels, codes of conduct, ratings (which overlap in parts) and with consumer information through the media. The general conditions for these private systems are again defined by government provisions, such as brand laws or regulations concerning bio labels.

Ethical reflection of labels

The labelling of goods and services is highly significant in ethical terms. Fundamental values (→ ch. 3) such as a fair assessment of quality and performance, environmental compatibility, fair procedure and transparency, the guarantee of genuine choice for consumers, and the assumption of responsibility for goods and services by all those involved along the trading chain requires information of this kind.

This ethically substantiated right to information, however, is coupled with the duty to read and be able to understand these labels. This is where many consumers reach their limits, particularly also in view of the increasing "jumble of labels". In addition, the costs of labelling and of the acquisition of information constitute a growing financial burden and thus a trade barrier for, say, SMEs and, in particular, for producers from developing countries; this is ethically disquieting since it factually excludes weak trading partners from the market. At the same time, the controlling effect of labels must not be overestimated.

The labelling instruments outlined below have different advantages and disadvantages from an ethical point of view and must therefore be assessed separately.

4.3 The ethics of labelling 2: Labelling provisions

Definition

Labelling provisions issued by a government or a community of countries define the data that must be disclosed for a product to be launched on the market. These data serve to inform consumers about aspects such as quality, health, safety, the environment, development or public morals.

Legal framework

Labelling provisions for (world) trade are to be found in the provisions of the GATT Treaty of 1994, particularly in the rules of the Agreement on Technical Barriers to Trade, including its Annex 3, "Code of Conduct for the Development, Adoption and Application of Standards", and they are also found in national legislation on technical trade barriers and consumer information laws. Government authorities also play a legal and coordinating role in relation to brands, labels and standards. In Switzerland, this has been specified as information and clarification, consultation and presentation, cooperation in the determination of order allocation criteria, internationally harmonized standards, mutual recognition of government labels, certification of labelling systems, ombudspersons for the label market, observation of the label market, public procurement system, financial support of private labelling systems, modification of the legal framework, and creation of government labels (*Bericht des Bundes über die Anerkennung und Förderung von Labels*, 2000, p. 3).

Ethical reflection: prerequisites for fairness

In ethical terms, transparent and checkable multilateral and national labelling provisions within the framework of a constitutional system are an important prerequisite for fair rules in trade, and for the guarantee of health, safety, environmental protection, fair development, and social acceptance.

**The ethics of labelling 3:
Brands**

Definition

A brand (legally called a trademark) is a symbol consisting of a word and/or an emblem identifying goods, services or companies; it stands for a corporate image as a whole. It guarantees constant or improved product characteristics. The brand is a mark that is registered or has common currency on the market.

Types and market significance of brands

- A manufacturer's brand is in the ownership of a producing company.
- A trader's brand is in the ownership of a trading company.
- A generic brand (no-name) is an umbrella brand for several groups of goods.

Brands are competitive instruments and, in particular, entail exclusive rights through brand protection. Trademarks have extended their market share ever since 1990, and their significance is on the increase. Their market shares according to groups of goods and operational form vary from country to country

Ethical reflection: cult brands

As a guarantee of standardized product quality, brands allow for an assessment of products and services according to fair performance, and to this extent must be considered ethically positive. Fair performance (→ ch. 3.2) is questionable, however, when prices are disproportionately high because of exclusive rights or their cult status. Brand products are particularly apt and prone to be turned into cult products if they do not satisfy a material need but become a substitute for religion, which must be rejected in ethical terms (cf. BOLZ/BOSSHART in their work on cult marketing: "The goods themselves become the strongest of all religions"). In this way, capitalism itself turns into a religion.

Examples of brands

Nescafé (Foodstuffs)
Manufacturer's brand

NESCAFÉ

Switcher (Textiles)
Trading brand

SWITCHER

Highscreen (Computers)
Generic brand

HIGHSCREEN

Examples of Labels

ISO 9000 (Quality management)
Private quality label

ISO

EU environmental emblem (Environment)
Government

BioSuisse (Environment)
Private product label

B I O
SUISSE

Max Havelaar (Fair trade, particularly food)
Private product label

MAX
HAVELAAR

STEP (Fair trade, carpets)
Private corporate label

STEP

→ Information about Swiss environmental and social labels, www.umweltschutz.ch/labelinfo
→ Global Ecolabelling Network, www.gen.gr.jp

Definition

A label (quality seal) is a voluntary designation of products or an identification of companies which contains information about products/product ranges, production methods or corporate standards. It often serves as a secondary brand on a product with a main brand in order to penetrate into additional (ethically motivated) market segments. It provides consumers with information about quality characteristics that go above and beyond legal provisions. Their distinctiveness from brands is fluid.

Types of labels

Labels vary according to subjects, criteria, and control modes.

- *Private labels* are only awarded by private subjects (NGOs, companies, industrial associations, etc.), which also determine the criteria and exercise their control mechanisms (e.g., Max Havelaar).
- *Government labels* are awarded by government authorities or supranational organizations, which determine the criteria and exercise their control mechanisms (e.g., EU environment emblem).
- *Product labels* identify individual products or product groups.
- *Corporate labels* identify companies or product ranges.
- *Pure quality labels* identify the (primarily technical) quality of products and companies.
- *Environment labels* (bio, eco, and energy labels) identify the environmental qualities of one or more production areas/production processes; they are of varying stringency.
- *Social labels* identify products or companies which create better working and pay conditions for all those who are involved in the production and trading processes, and make provisions for redundancy schemes through higher product prices or contributions.
- *Transition labels* are process-oriented labels, designating a company in transition (→ ch. 2.6). Their advantage is that the first step towards change in the direction of ethically responsible trade is rewarded even though the ethical criteria have not yet been satisfied. To be awarded this label, a company must submit a goal attainment schedule. The disadvantage is that ethics in the transition label process may lead to a dilution of ethical standards and confuse consumers.

Substance

Comprehensive environment labels are based of life-cycle analyses (e.g., *Blauer Engel*), others on individual product or service characteristics (e.g., "FHC-free", or the environment emblems for tourism).

A majority of social labels are based on the minimum standards of the International Labour Organization (ILO) as they are stipulated in the seven core conventions: the ban on forced labour (ILO Conventions 29 and 105), freedom to associate in trade unions and protection of their rights (87 and 135), equal pay for equal work and the prohibition of discrimination (100/111), and the protection of the minimum working age and a ban on child labour (138). Pay is not fixed in the social labels, but the criterion usually applied is that it is above the legal minimum wage and must cover the subsistence minimum. This sounds little but in many developing countries is a definite step forward in comparison with practice. Brand products or products in general use are more suitable for labels than generica or very expensive products.

Ethical reflection: examine labels carefully

Labels set ethical standards as criteria for orientation. They express the fact that ethical aspirations go above and beyond what is legally binding. They provide consumers with a choice, within the framework of market mechanisms, of what is ethically more valuable, thus enabling them to influence the market, at least to a limited extent. Labels are trendsetters and therefore often precursors of legally binding provisions. Because they are difficult to control, labels can as a rule only assess parts of the production chain from raw materials to final sale and product disposal. The more comprehensive this chain is, the more ethically qualified the label. Its ethical quality further depends on the motives behind its origin, on the holistic approach of its substance (does it concern individual details or has it been formulated with a sense of universal responsibility?), on the participatory development process (decreed from above or shared by all those concerned?), on the seriousness of compliance and monitoring by auditors and by the market. "Cheap labels" which do not satisfy these requirements can be abused as pure instruments of PR.

4.6 The ethics of labelling 5: Codes of conduct

Definition

A code of conduct (*code de conduite, Verhaltenskodex*) is a voluntary agreement on the rules of conduct, involving duties and rights, of institutions such as companies, government authorities, NGOs, churches or of private individuals inside these institutions. Codes of conduct vary in their binding nature and scope and are often precursors of legislation.

Types of codes of conduct

Various types of codes of conduct (CCs) can be distinguished according to width and depth:

- comprehensive CCs of international organizations (e.g., UN code for transnational companies);
- limited CCs of international organizations (e.g., ILO Declaration concerning Multinational Enterprises and Social Policy);
- product-specific CCs of international organizations (e.g., the WHO's infant formula code and the FAO's pesticide code);
- CCs of individual industries (e.g., oil industry);
- CCs for professions (e.g., researchers or civil servants);
- corporate CC for the company as a whole or for a single division or product range (e.g., Nike);
- NGOs' CCs for their own activities;
- specimen codes for companies (e.g., Clean Clothes, benchmarks or the Interfaith Centers on Corporate Responsibility);
- NGOs' CCs for companies of a particular industry (e.g., Clean Clothes Code of development organizations for the textile industry).

Diversity and substance

As with labels, codes of conduct vary widely with regard to their provisions, target groups, development process and monitoring mechanism. What was said about the substance of the labels largely applies to codes, too. Corporate codes often primarily concern the conduct of personnel towards the company itself (loyalty, compliance with the law, prohibition of competition and corruption), while codes for more than one firm pay more attention to the companies' social, ecological and development-political responsibility. In a 1998 survey, the International Labour Organization (ILO) examined over 200 codes and labels with regard to labour standards. The seven ILO core standards, which were declared binding on all

---

Examples of different codes of conduct

Novartis	*Corporate code*, 1999, limited to personnel conduct. Constituent part of the group's employment contract.
Oil companies	*Industrial code* for the oil and gas industry, drafted 1999 by "Brot für die Welt".
EU	*Multilateral code* of the EU for multinational companies operating in developing countries (1999, in planning phase).
CCC	Clean Clothes Codex, 1991ff: *model code* for fair trade in textiles, created for textile and clothing companies by the Clean Clothes Campaign.
STEP	*Code with label*, 1995, for fair trade in carpets, created by the Swiss STEP foundation for its licensees, combined with a corporate label for points of sale.
Benchmarks	Principles for Global Corporate Responsibility. *Benchmarks* for Measuring Business Performance, 1995, developed by three church institutions in the US, Canada and Ireland. Responsibility towards all the stakeholders.
ICGN	*Association code* for investors of the International Corporate Governance Network (ICGN), the most powerful Anglo-Saxon investment fund, and British insurers.
Foodstuffs	*One-issue "Code of conduct* regarding the right to food", developed in 1997 by NGOs on behalf of the NGO Forum of the World Food Summit, for government and companies.
Administration	Code of Conduct for Public Servants (1998?) by the Committee for *Public Services* of the South African government.

The addresses for the codes will be found in the Appendix to this book.

member states in the *ILO Declaration concerning the Core Labour Standards* in June 1998, were not completely contained in a third of the above-mentioned codes.

Labels and codes of conduct complement each other: whereas codes are basically companies' self-imposed obligations to observe certain standards, labels inform consumers about precisely those standards.

Ethical reflection: examine codes carefully

Codes of conduct set ethical standards as criteria for orientation. Their ethical quality depends on the motives behind their origins (e. g., encouragement of ethical responsibility, or preclusion of stricter laws?), on the holistic approach of their substance (do they concern individual details, or have they been formulated with a sense of universal responsibility?), on the participatory development process (decreed from above, or shared by all those concerned?), on the seriousness of compliance, monitoring and verification by auditors and by the market.

The rapid expansion of codes of conduct since the 1990s – in parallel with the thrust of liberalization and globalization – reveals the extent to which global government authorities that are still being set up should provide globally operating companies with regulations. In its study concerning codes of conduct, the European Commission stated bluntly: "The proliferation of codes of conduct reflects the failure of governments and international organizations to enforce minimum standards." (1999, p. 7). Voluntary codes are ethically valuable if they implement ethical standards more quickly and more effectively than government regulations, and if they constitute precursors of standards to be implemented under international law. They are ethically dubious, however, if they aim at the prevention of such standards or serve as smokescreens. Although the actual effect of these codes should not be overestimated, they should still not be underestimated as an opportunity for responsibility.

Monitoring systems

Model A) In-house monitoring

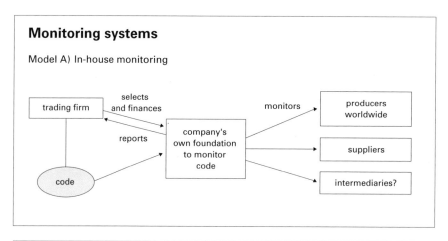

Model B) Independent tripartite monitoring

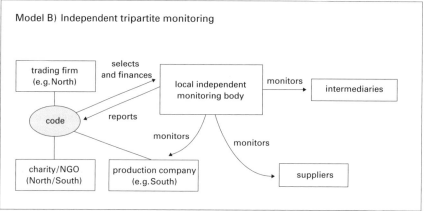

Modell C) Independent standardized monitoring

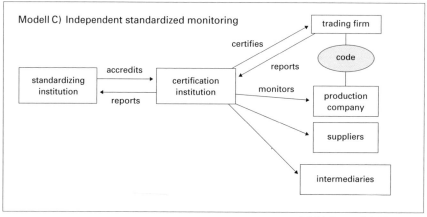

© Stückelberger: Global Trade Ethics

Definition

Controlling is an instrument widely used in companies for making comparisons between actual and planned results throughout the management cycle. It is meant to take its bearings from profits, costs, quality, customers and – this is new – ethics.

Internal monitoring (continual review) describes the process of regular information-gathering to examine the compliance of the standards and criteria of labels and codes of conduct.

External monitoring or *verification* describes the process of regular external assessment (auditing by auditors) of whether internal monitoring is complete, appropriate, has been carried out on schedule and been accompanied by the necessary measures. Monitoring and verification are part of controlling as a whole.

Types and examples of monitoring

Private monitoring

- *Corporate monitoring*
  such as the SOCAM foundation established in 1996 and financed by the clothing group C&A to monitor its own corporate code ($\rightarrow$ graph, model A).
- *Independent self-appointed monitoring*
  such as the Interagency Group on Breastfeeding Monitoring (IGBM) monitors the 1981 WHO Code of Marketing of Breast-milk Substitutes; it was set up by churches and NGOs in England in 1994 and is financed by these.
- *Independent tripartite monitoring (foundation model)*
  such as Monitoring of the social clause of Migros-Del Monte Switzerland-Philippines since 1993. Independent Philippine monitoring body instituted by the Swiss trading chain Migros, Del Monte Philippines, and the Swiss charities Bread for all and Fastenopfer (cf. graph, model B).
- *Independent monitoring prescribed by a standard institute*
  such as Standard SA8000, monitored by certification institution authorized to do so ($\rightarrow$ graph, model C).

Government monitoring

- *Voluntary multilateral or national monitoring*
  such as European Community Eco-Management and Audit Scheme (EMAS) for industrial companies in Europe, since 1993.

- *Binding multilateral or national monitoring*
  such as the monitoring of the 1981 WHO Code of Marketing of Breast-milk
  Substitutes by WHO and UNICEF.

Ethical reflection: aspire to credible monitoring

A company's compliance with codes of conduct and ethical labels can enhance its
ethical seriousness and that of its brands to a considerable extent. The prerequisite
for this is a serious monitoring of all these brands, labels and codes.

Ethical criteria (→ fundamental values in chapter 3) for credible monitoring include the following:

- *Trust* in trade relations admits of transparent monitoring and does not run
  counter to them.
- The *participation* of various qualified interest groups, of those who are monitored (employees other than management, management, staff committees,
  trade unions), and foreign monitors together with local ones.
- *Independence* through the necessary access to information and through surprise
  visits and scheduled visits.
- *Transparency* through the publication of procedures and, where possible, the
  results (i.e., without confidential corporate information).
- *Life enhancement* through a reviewable plan for corrective measures in the service of social and ecological aims, (only) afterwards any possible sanctions such
  as media report, withdrawal of the label or code, or termination of trade relations.
- *Fair distribution* through cost-efficient monitoring and the fair distribution of
  monitoring costs.
- *Fair participation* through public and private development programmes to
  establish local monitoring systems in the environment of those who are affected,
  to reinforce democracy and media freedom.

4.8 Marketing ethics 1: Statistics

Trade statistics: an instrument of planning and power

Market research is an important part of marketing, and it depends on market and trade statistics. Plans drawn up by companies, government and NGOs take their bearings to a large extent from statistics, whose significance is even more on the increase in an economy that is globalized, dominated by IT and characterized by an extreme division of labour. Access to the relevant information is an element of planning and power. Disraeli may have said "There are three kinds of lies: lies, damned lies and statistics" a long time ago, but the mistrust of statistics is as rife as ever.

Ethical reflection of market and trade statistics

Statistics are vital to the planning of responsible trade. However, they are always based on value-related preliminary decisions, which means that they are basically not value-free even though they are established clearly and objectively within the framework of these preliminary decisions.

- The selection of data implies value judgments as to which data are regarded as valuable and useful, and so they derive from a certain value system. Thus, say, the gender of employees in an industry in an industrialized nation is considered a focal point in view of the efforts made in the field of gender equality, whereas religious affiliation is not taken into account. In countries such as India or Iran, this might well be the other way round if they were able to choose their statistics freely, without the international pressure of trading partners or supranational institutions. The consequence for business ethics is that the value basis of statistics should be made transparent.
- There are also data which are not taken into account because they are too delicate in political or economic terms, such as environmental and social data. Others are taken into account but not made accessible to the general public. Yet other statistics are inaccurate owing to unqualified personnel or lack of funds, or they have been falsified by corruption in the country in question or by the black market. The consequence for business ethics is that published and, in particular, missing and unpublished statistics must be checked for their ethical implications.

4.9 Marketing ethics 2: Communication and advertising

International Code of Advertising Practice

International Chamber of Commerce ICC, 1997
Extract from 23 articles

[...]

Basic principles

Article 1

All advertising should be legal, decent, honest and truthful. Every advertisement should be prepared with a due sense of social responsibility and should conform to the principles of fair competition, as generally accepted in business. No advertisement should be such as to impair public confidence in advertising.

Social responsibility

Article 4

1. Advertisements should not condone any form of discrimination, including that based upon race, national origin, religion, sex or age, nor should they in any way undermine human dignity.
2. Advertisements should not without justifiable reason play on fear.
3. Advertisements should not appear to condone or incite violence, nor to encourage unlawful or reprehensible behaviour.
4. Advertisements should not play on superstition.

Truthful presentation

Article 5

1. Advertisements should not contain any statement or visual presentation which directly or by implication, omission, ambiguity or exaggerated claim is likely to mislead the consumer, in particular with regard to
   a. characteristics such as: nature, composition, method and date of manufacture, range of use, efficiency and performance, quantity, commercial or geographical origin or environmental impact;
   b. the value of the product and the total price actually to be paid;
   c. delivery, exchange, return, repair and maintenance;
   d. terms of guarantee;
   e. copyright and industrial property rights such as patents, trade marks, designs and models and trade names;
   f. official recognition or approval, awards of medals, prizes and diplomas;
   g. the extent of benefits for charitable causes.
2. Advertisements should not misuse research results or quotations from technical and scientific publications. Statistics should not be so presented as to exaggerate the validity of advertising claims. Scientific terms should not be used to falsely ascribe scientific validity to advertising claims.

Source: ICC 1997

Definitions

Marketing, i.e., that part of a company which plans and operates the necessary activities on the sales market, involves market research ($\rightarrow$ ch. 4.8), product design and pricing ($\rightarrow$ ch. 6.1), public relations and advertising ($\rightarrow$ ch. 4.9), and sales and distribution ($\rightarrow$ ch. 4.10). *Public relations (PR)* involves the activities with which an institution seeks to win over the general public for its work and aims. *Advertising* is part of PR and attempts to exert a targeted, intentional and non-coercive influence on customers for the purpose of selling goods and services, by means of individual advertising (company) or collective advertising (e.g., an association advertising the products of a particular industry).

Ethical reflection: marketing coherence

The various instruments of communication – personal sale, sales promotion, sales outlet design, advertising, sponsorship and PR – must be coherent with regard to their ethical message and in the different countries. Double standards are ethically inadmissible. If the seriousness of ethical efforts is important in the context of labels ($\rightarrow$ chs. 4.2 – 4.7), it is equally important in advertising and PR, as well as in a company's environmental and social reports. With increasing frequency, top managers themselves become "brand products", labels, and communicators of credibility. Whatever is promised by a label must be congruent with advertising and shop design. Advertising with ethics as an "additional benefit" for consumers must be supported if its promises are consistent with factual ethical conduct.

The most current reproaches levelled at advertising must be reconsidered in ethical terms again and again, and be refuted by advertising practice itself: untruthfulness, consumer manipulation, artificial creation of needs, exploitation of emotions, advertising for harmful products, morally offensive representations (sensations, clichés, misogyny, racism), commercialization of the world in which we live, or harassment by advertising. Codes such as the International Code on Advertising Practice of the International Chamber of Commerce are useful approaches which, in the view of new challenges such as e-commerce, must be developed further.

Internet connections

per 1000 inhabitants in the world's regions, end of 1998

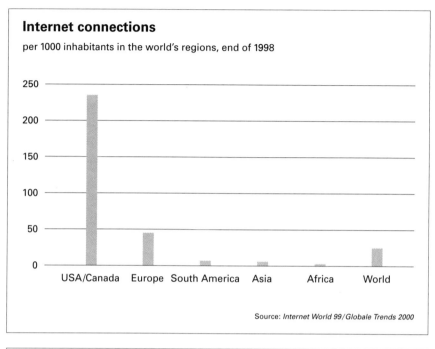

Source: *Internet World 99/Globale Trends 2000*

Boom in e-commerce

Internet turnover in billion US dollars

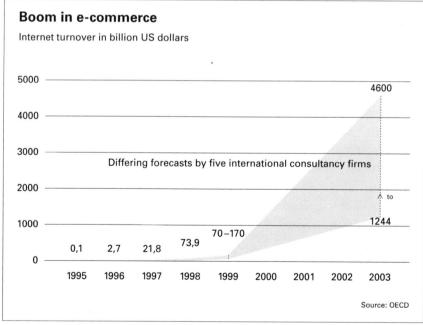

Differing forecasts by five international consultancy firms

4600

to

1244

0,1   2,7   21,8   73,9   70–170

Source: OECD

Definition

E-commerce (electronic commerce) is a modern method of trade which makes use of computer networks to address the requirements of organizations and consumers in order to cut costs, to improve the quality of goods and services, to reduce lead times, and thus to gain a competitive edge. E-commerce is tantamount to electronic shopping.

Enormous development and change of trade

The Internet has become the world's biggest marketplace. An Internet presence is a must today, particularly for import-/export-oriented companies. Business-to-business sales still produce far more turnover than business-to-consumer sales. The salesperson/customer relationship has been turned around in that it is not the salesperson who looks for the customer through marketing, but the customer who looks for the advertisements, the manufacturer and the most favourably priced distribution channel for a certain product. E-commerce is important for sales, but especially also for customer service, information gathering and transport logistics. Moreover, it alters the structure of firms in the direction of virtual company integration.

E-commerce = ethical commerce?

In ethical terms, the three aims defined above, and their feasibility, must be subjected to a holistic review. *Cost efficiency*, i.e., an economical use of resources, is ethically positive (provided the true costs are known in that external costs are internalized). The greatly varying Internet costs, however, exclude large parts of the world population, thus widening the gap between rich and poor – in Bangladesh, for instance, the costs for one single Internet connection would feed a family for a whole year! The question as to whether *quality* is improved remains open. *Speedy delivery* can be life-enhancing, but stretches the physical and ecological limits of transport capacities, thus endangering the fundamental value of sustainability. The *ethical criteria* of labels and codes must also be applied to e-commerce (adaptation of the workplace, working conditions; e. g., as regards working on Sundays with 365-day on-line shopping, on-line company and product ratings). Information technologies, too, must be democratically regulated and controlled.

Examples of ratings for consumers

The Company Tester
Product and company tests of 75 food and beverage companies in Germany according to 12 groups of social and ecological criteria (openness of information, consumer interests, employees, disabled people, Third World, new Länder and foreigners, promotion of women, commitment to the environment, genetic technology, animal protection, donations), developed by the Institut für Markt-Umwelt-Gesellschaft (imug) together with consumer associations, environmental organizations and charities, published in 1995.

Shopping for a Better World
Product rating published in 1998 (millions of copies sold!) for consumers in the USA, according to eight groups of criteria (promotion of the environment, of women, of minorities, of the family, of the community, donations, working conditions, information conduct), developed by the Council on Economic Priorities (CEP), a private research institution in New York.

Examples of ratings for investors

Dow Jones Sustainability Index
This index, which has been in existence since 1999, rates companies quoted on the stock exchange according to a few hundred sustainability criteria. The index is drawn up by the rating agency Sustainability Asset Management (SAM) in Zurich and published by Dow Jones (New York).

The Corporate Report Card
A rating of 250 US companies according to eight groups of "Shopping" criteria (cf. above) conducted by the CEP since 1987: Corporate Conscience Awards.

For further information, cf. Literature and Internet addresses below.

Definition

In banking, *rating* is the classification of debtors in the international credit systems, either as a national rating or an issuer rating. In ethical market research, it is now used as an ethical product, company and country rating, which rates company, products and countries according to standardized and usually social/ecological criteria and grades them on a scale. It serves as a decision-making aid for consumers (advice on responsible shopping), for investors (stock-exchange indices and advice on ethical investment) and for companies (choice of trading, production and service partners). Individual rating institutions confer awards and promotional prizes as incentives for ethical trade.

Development

Rating is particularly widespread in the industrialized nations: USA and Canada, in Central and Northern Europe, in Japan, and increasingly also in the rest of Europe. Global rating criteria are being discussed; rating agencies from transition and development countries are still not sufficiently involved.

Ethical reflection: the criteria are decisive

Company and product ratings according to ethical criteria are effective market-economic decision-making instruments for participants in the market. The more the economy is globalized, based on the division of labour, and characterized by complexity, the more heavily investors, producers and consumers will depend on it. This partial delegation of responsibility reveals the great responsibility of the rating agencies. It does not, however, relieve individuals of the obligation to scrutinize the criteria on which the ratings are based, because they are always selective, and their selection and weighting derives from a certain code of values. When a company's environmental conduct is rated, for instance, it is often only its environmental management that is taken into account, whereas the environmental consequences of its products are disregarded. Thus the Corporate Report Card (on the left); the environmental conduct of the oil company Texaco received an above-average rating of B, yet the CO_2 emissions of its product, oil, are not taken into account. Generally speaking, existing ethical ratings attach too little weight to global development questions as opposed to environmental and social conduct ($\rightarrow$ ch. 6.14, "Ethical investments").

Examples of global trade campaigns

Child labour

The *Global March against Child Labour* consisted of marches organized on all the continents, which reached their final destination, the headquarters of the International Labour Organization (ILO) in Geneva in 1997. It is remarkable that this campaign was launched in the South (India) and received particular backing in Asia, Latin America, and Africa.

Textiles

The Europe-wide *Clean Clothes Campaign* for a fair, "clean" textile trade, i.e. fair working conditions in low-pay countries, with producing and trading companies of the textile and clothing industry being offered an opportunity to sign a code.

Land mines

The *International Campaign to Ban Landmines* for a ban on the production of, trade in, and dissemination and use of land mines has been active since 1992. It has been promoting the governments' political will to sign and ratify the 1997 Mine Ban Treaty (Ottawa Convention). In 1997, the campaign was awarded the Nobel Peace Prize.

Debt remission

Jubilee 2000: a worldwide campaign with particular support in developing countries for the remission of debts (trade in capital) with a petition of 17 million signatures and a promise of additional debt remission by the Cologne G8 Summit in 1999.

Definition

Campaigns are activities of limited duration which seek to attain certain objectives such as a change in the conduct of a target group by making the general public or certain target groups sensitive to an issue and by mobilising them. As a rule, the driving forces behind campaigns are organized associations, NGOs, networks, or increasingly international ad hoc coalitions of organizations.

Types, opportunities and limits

There are various types of campaigns: they may be aimed a products, like that against footballs made in Pakistan before the World Cup; at issues, like that against child labour; at companies, like that against Monsanto and its genetically modified sweet-corn; at countries, like those against trade with South Africa at the time of apartheid; and they are national and, increasingly, international (→ box on the left). They usually start off national or international political endeavours and processes, and they are paid considerable attention by the media. This means that they reinforce companies' readiness to sign ethical standards with regard to trade. When the economic competition within the industry becomes fierce, however, or when the pressure exerted by the campaign is reduced, this readiness may diminish. The real change potential thus depends on the interaction between political, economic and media-related agents.

Ethical reflection: truthful criticism

Campaigns must be truthful and provide fair information about the targets of their criticism. Any improvements that have been achieved must be reported on and, at the same time, be critically monitored (→ ch. 4.7), although this usually leads to a second phase in the wake of the campaign, which is by definition limited in time. An ethics which focuses on responsibility and takes the consequences of trade seriously, must look at the overall effects of the campaign: the positive or negative effects on the various trading partners involved (e.g., on jobs) and on the opportunities for cooperation with these partners, i.e., the possible strategies and phases of criticism, of resistance, of dialogue and of cooperation must be examined as early as the planning stage of the campaign.

UN sanctions

Pursuant to Articles 4 and 41 of the UN Charter, the UN Security Council may call on member states to take measures (without the use of arms) to preserve or restore peace and security; these measures are called sanctions. Since the establishment of the UN, it has imposed sanctions against 15 countries:

Country	Year	Extent	as at 2000
Ethiopia	2000	Partial embargo	in force
Afghanistan	1999	Partial embargo	in force
Angola	1993, 97–2000	Partial embargo	in force
Eritrea	2000	Partial embargo	in force
Haiti	1993	Partial embargo	lifted
Iraq	1990–2000	Various embargos	in force
Yugoslavia	1991	Full embargo	lifted
Republik Yugoslavia/ Kosovo	1998	Partial embargo	in force
Liberia	1992	Partial embargo	in force
Libya	1992	Full embargo	suspended
Rwanda	1994	Partial embargo	partly lifted
Sierra Leone	1997	Partial embargo	lifted
	2000	Partial embargo	in force
Somalia	1992	Partial embargo	in force
South Africa	1979	Full embargo	lifted
South Rhodesia	1966	Full embargo	lifted
Sudan	1996	Partial embargo	not executed

Source: Uno, 2000 (www.un.org/news/ossg/sanction). Author's layout

In many cases, these were primarily arms embargos. Such embargos also exist in the EU, in 2000 against Afghanistan, Burma, China, Congo/Zaire, Nigeria, Sierra Leone, and Sudan.
An example: since 1993, German companies have not been allowed to declare boycotts through participation in boycotts against third-party countries.

© Stückelberger: Global Trade Ethics

Definition

A boycott is the severance of trade or consumer relations, where import/export or consumption, respectively, are interrupted until such time as an economic, political or ideational aim has been attained with regard to the economic subject targeted by the boycott.

Types of boycotts

Government boycotts
- multilateral general trade boycott, usually imposed by the UN General Assembly against a country to achieve certain political aims (sanctions, art. 41, UN Charter);
- bilateral general or selective trade boycott against a country or company to achieve certain political aims.

Private boycotts, coordinated by NGOs or campaign organizations,
and executed by consumers:
- private consumer boycott against a company to make it change its conduct in a certain way;
- private consumer boycott against a product or a product characteristic, such as "contains FHC", of various producers to make them change that particular product;
- private consumer boycott against products from a certain country to achieve a product change or certain political aims.

Ethical reflection: value judgment on effect/sacrifice

Political and economic studies of boycotts as an instrument to enforce changes of conduct conclude that their effectiveness varies, but is limited in a majority of cases. In general trade boycotts against countries, a value judgment (→ ch. 2.4) must be made between the odds for achieving the aim (in opposition of governments) and the minimization of sacrifices (to be borne by the population). Justice in terms of equal treatment is violated in cases where trade boycotts against countries tend to be imposed against weaker trading partners and hardly ever against strong ones. Private consumer boycotts are more concerted but less effective. Product ratings (→ ch. 4.11) are indirect appeals for product boycotts ("Don't buy x."), with the emphasis placed on an ethically more positive incentive ("Buy y instead of x.") rather than on sanctions.

Instruments of trade policy

National instruments		Bilateral instruments		Multilateral/international instruments	
Types	→ Aims	Types	→ Aims	Types	→ Aims
Tariffs	→ Price increase	Trade agreements	→ Long-term regulation of trade relations	GATT/WTO	→ Reduction of tariff and trade banners
Subsidies	→ Price reduction				
Contingents	→ Limitation of volumes	Trade treaties	→ Short-term agreement of specific measures	EU tariff and trade treaties	→ Mutuals preferences
Import/ export bans	→ Prevention of economic relations			Raw material treaties	→ Agreements on goods between producer and user countries
Non-tariff trade barriers	→ Arbitrary/ covert obstruction				

Source: Jahrmann 1998, p. 35

Example: environmental treaties relevant to trade

(selection)

- Vienna Convention on the Protection of the Ozone Layer
  www.unep.ch/ozone
- Basel Convention on the Control of Transboundary Movements
  of Hazardous Wastes and their Disposal
  www.basel.int
- Convention of Biological Diversity (Biodiversity Convention)
  www.biodiv.org
- Framework Convention on Climate Change
  www.unfccc.de
- Convention on Persistent Organic Pollutants
  irptc.unep.ch/pops
- Convention of International Trade in Endangered Species
  in Wild Fauna and Flora (CITES)
  www.cites.org

From investment protection to the protection of human rights

The significance of international treaties relevant to international law is continuing to increase in a globalized world. Many of them are political framework conditions and, as such, directly or indirectly relevant to trade. The following are some of the most important.

- *World trade:* the rules provided by WTO/GATT, which apply to about 95 per cent of the entire world trade (→ ch. 5.22); the programmes of UNCTAD, particularly for developing countries; the UN Charter with the countries' economic rights and duties.
- *Regional trade:* regional trade agreements and free trade areas such as the EU, NAFTA, APEC, ECOWAS (→ ch. 5.21)
- *Investment:* the Multilateral Agreement on Investments (MAI), which was launched by the OECD and has so far failed.
- *Development financing:* IMF/World Bank.
- *Sustainable development:* Agenda 21 of the UN World Conference on Environment and Development, many environmental treaties (→ previous page)
- *Human rights:* 1966 UN Pacts on human rights (→ ch. 6.18).
- *Labour rights:* numerous ILO conventions (→ ch. 5.23).

Ethical reflection: aspire to coherence

One burning challenge resulting from the increasing significance and number of international treaties is the power struggle between the various international organizations and the priority of their treaties. The ethical task consists in the mediation between competing aims and values. In such value clashes, the methods of the value judgment, preference rules (→ ch. 2.4) and compromise (→ ch. 2.5) must be applied. Just as, in the service of credible politics, coherence must be aspired to between national policy areas, coherence must also be sought between the various international treaties, particularly between global investment, trade, social, environment and human rights policies, although this will be even more difficult. A first step in this direction is the determination of the value clashes and the recognition that all the various values are basically equal, and that they need not subject themselves to economic aims from the start. A trade policy without contradictions in not possible, a trade policy with fewer contradictions is.

South: populations for, governments against

Survey among 82 non-governmental organizations and trade unions
from 27 countries, 65 of which were from 24 developing countries

Should social clauses be introduced
in international trade?

Should social clauses be linked to
sanctions? (responses only from
NGO/trade unions from the South)

1% with no reply   7% no

92% yes

6% with no reply   4% no

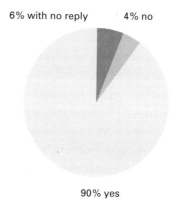

90% yes

Source: Egger/Schümperli 1996, pp. 3 and 24

Proponents of social/environmental clauses in trade agreements
- Most governments of industrial nations, including the EU and USA
- A large number of employees in developing countries,
  and of employers and employees in industrial nations.
- A large number of charities/civilian society in the North

Opponents of social/environment clauses in trade agreements
- Most governments of developing countries
- Most employers in developing countries
- A small number of employees in developing countries

Different views
In the WTO Conference of Ministers, the supreme decision-making body, social and
environmental clauses have so far found no majority. However, the ILO was asked in
Singapore in 1998 to develop proposals for minimum standards. Economists and many
international organizations hold different views on the effectiveness of such clauses.

Definition

Clauses are special provisions of a restrictive nature which are attached to or integrated into an agreement (e.g. Israel's black-list clauses in certificates of origin for exports into Islamic countries). Social and environment clauses in trade agreements call for minimum standards in respect of working conditions in production and services (e.g., ILO core labour standards) and for the protection of the non-human environment, respectively.

Arguments for

- Human rights must be respected regardless of a country's economic development and production level.
- Liberalized world trade requires a social and ecological framework.
- Social and ecological dumping endangers social peace and the sustainable safeguard of basic necessities.

Arguments against

- Social and environment clauses are demanded by the North with protectionist intent, and disadvantage the South.
- They are trade barriers and thus in contradiction to free trade.
- They are unsuitable for the removal of competitive distortions.
- Their effect is primarily limited to the area of exports.

Ethical reflection: means are negotiable, aim is not

Ethical minimum standards (we are not talking about maximum standards!) are not negotiable since, needless to say, they protect the fundamental rights and the basic dignity of people and nature. Ethical business exceeds more than minimum requirements. Whether clauses in trade agreements are a suitable instrument for this, however, is a question of weighing up the means. In terms of an ethics of responsibility, the means must be measured with regard to efficiency and feasibility. If social and environment clauses are rejected, alternatives must be shown regarding how minimum standards are respected in trade activities.

The 1998 ILO Declaration concerning the Core Labour Standards (→ ch. 5.23), which is binding on virtually all the countries, could factually assume the function of social clauses if it were taken seriously.

4.16 World trade policy 3: Instruments of preference

Definition

Instruments of preference guarantee the selective preferential treatment of trading partners for the compensation for disparate basic conditions or for concerted trade control. They can also be granted when the fundamental equal treatment of trading partners (WTO rules) is recognized.

Examples

Tariff preferences (preferential tariffs) grant partner countries advantages through lower or suspended tariffs for imports from these countries. They were very important for the export opportunities of poor developing countries; in the wake of trade liberalization, however, they are losing some of their significance because the aim is the general reduction of tariffs. Yet they are still a valid instrument.

WTO Special and Differential Treatment intends to provide developing countries with a certain compensation for the very unequal basic conditions; e.g., through extended transition periods for the adaptation of their trade to the WTO rules, or through technical aid. The instrument is important in terms of development policy but factually too weak for actual effects.

Ethical reflection: equalize inequality

Preferences ultimately concern the relationship between distributive and commutative justice. The former provides everyone with the same (WTO: one member state, one vote), the latter provides everyone with their due (according to performance or need). Thus preferences compensate at least slightly for the disparate conditions from which trade relations start. Social and environment clauses in trade preferences (as introduced in the EU tariff preferences) are positive incentives and to this extent more effective than negative sanctions.

5

Agents of ethical responsibility in trade

All the participants in an economy are potential agents of ethically responsible trade. As chapters 1–4 have dealt with the methods, values and instruments, this chapter will now account for people; i.e., for the subjects who bear responsibility. This concerns both the ethics of private individuals and the ethics of institutions; i.e., the business represented by and in institutions (→ ch.1.4). Institutional ethics concerns institutions as agents with their objectives, exertion of influence, means of power, and legal and economic conditions. These will be explained with the help of typical examples.

The agents in respect of a certain institution include all the interested groups (stakeholders): private individuals, groups or institutions which influence, or are influenced by, an organization/company, be this internally (e.g. personnel) or externally (e.g. shareholders, local community, suppliers). To the extent to which *stakeholders* or *shareholders* assume a share in the responsibility of an institution's ethical orientation, they become careholders; i.e., responsible, caring participants.

The question as to the agents' responsibility is at the same time the question as to their power or counterpower. Power and counterpower are often seen as contrary to ethical conduct. The opposite is true: ethics requires power so that responsibility can be assumed, and it requires counterpower so that it can be controlled (→ Power/responsibility in chapter 3.10). Theological business ethics conceives of this power/responsibility as a response to the word of God and His creative love; i.e., as responsible stewardship of the earth which God lent to man to dwell in and "to dress it and to keep it" (Gen. 2:15), as we were told to do in the history of creation.

Proponents of ethical action

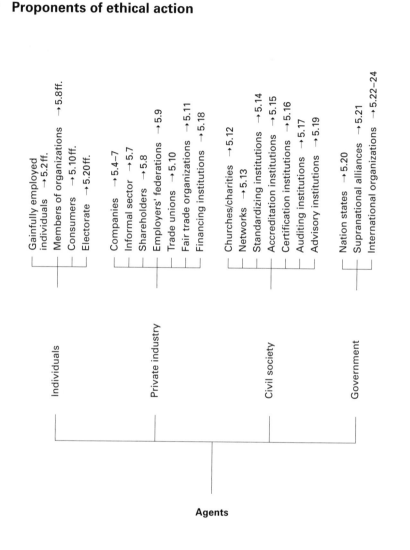

Individuals
- Gainfully employed individuals →5.2ff.
- Members of organizations →5.8ff.
- Consumers →5.10ff.
- Electorate →5.20ff.

Private industry
- Companies →5.4–7
- Informal sector →5.7
- Shareholders →5.8
- Employers' federations →5.9
- Trade unions →5.10
- Fair trade organizations →5.11
- Financing institutions →5.18

Civil society
- Churches/charities →5.12
- Networks →5.13
- Standardizing institutions →5.14
- Accreditation institutions →5.15
- Certification institutions →5.16
- Auditing institutions →5.17
- Advisory institutions →5.19

Government
- Nation states →5.20
- Supranational alliances →5.21
- International organizations →5.22–24

Agents

All the economic subjects are potential agents of ethically responsible trade.
Various institutions must be allocated to more than one area.

© Stückelberger: Global Trade Ethics

Four categories of agents

A distinction is made between four categories (→ table), which are represented by examples (not exhaustive; (→ chs. 5.2 – 24).

- *Individuals* usually provide the decisive stimulus for ethical innovations in institutions.
- *Private institutions* comprise a wide variety of heterogeneous forms of profit-oriented institutions, their owners and of economic interest groups.
- *Civil society institutions* comprise a wide variety of heterogeneous forms of non-profit-oriented social, ecological and ideational institutions which are independent of the public and private sectors.
- *Government institutions* comprise nation states and federations to which nation states relinquish part of their competencies, and international organizations such as the UN system.
- Many institutions are *mixed forms* of these categories.

Four types of value-creating institutions

- *Standard-determining institutions* determine legal or private standards and values (governments, standardizing institutions, churches/religious communities, increasingly also the media).
- *Standard-implementing institutions* are all the institutions in their respective sectors.
- *Standard-enforcing institutions* are public or private institutions with the authority to impose legal, military, moral or economic sanctions, often identical with the standard-determining institutions.
- *Standard-developing institutions* are public or private institutions for the further development of standards and values, in evolutionary processes often identical with the standard-determining institutions or established in opposition to them, in revolutionary processes represented by the opposition.

Specific ethical power, limit, responsibility

Each institutional form has specific possibilities of power and responsibilities for the promotion of ethical trade, but also specific limits. This chapter will have a look at both these aspects with the aim of finding the optimal and most effective institutional form and level for each business-ethical problem solution.

Types of ethical conduct in management

Form of perception Problem consciousness	Culture-oriented perception of the economy	Culture-oriented perception of the economy
Harmony-conscious	Economists	Conventionalists
Conflict-conscious	Reformers	Idealists

Source: Ulrich/Thielemann 1992, 26

Ulrich and Thielemann of the Institute for Business Ethics in St. Gallen (Switzerland) developed four types of ethical conduct of managers, for which they gathered empirical evidence in interviews with top managers. In the form of perception, some experience the anonymous structures of the economy as particularly impressive whereas others see ethics integrated into economic life as a matter of course. With regard to conflict consciousness, some discern harmony between ethics and success while others regularly see conflicts. Empirically, 75% are rated economists; the reformers constitute the type of the New Entrepreneur.

- For the economist, the market mechanisms with the principle of competition automatically lead to ethically correct trade.

- For the conventionalist, corporate ethics is a matter of course since social morals also apply in the economy.

- For the idealist, the conflict can be solved by special efforts in a change of consciousness, while the system need not be changed.

- For the reformer, however, an ethically oriented change and a reform of the structure of factual economic constraints is necessary.

© Stückelberger: Global Trade Ethics

Individuals as the driving force

Individuals, in their capacities as gainfully employed persons, consumers, members of associations, clubs, churches and action groups, as well as voting citizens or members of parliament, are the central agents of ethical business. Despite all the institutional standards and constraints, it is individuals who shape institutions and drive their ethical conduct. Together, they constitute what could be called *Ethical Corporate Identity* (ECI).

Management ethics

Managers are particularly important as ethical innovators (or preventers). The focus is therefore on the ethical responsibility of managers. In my own experience of cooperation between companies, NGOs and government authorities in connection with ethical business, I keep noticing that it is often one single personality in a strategically favourable position who is able to move an institution. Often, people like this are senior managers capable of skilfully persuading top management, and managers from sensitive departments that are particularly strongly exposed to ethical pressure from the general public.

Specific responsibility: career with ethics

The greater one's power, the greater one's ethical responsibility towards the various stakeholders. Here, the personal question as to career and ethics plays a central role: the proposal to introduce a code of conduct or a social label in a company may promote or hinder one's career. A personal and institutional credibility strategy implies that ethics is not used opportunistically and for specific details, but as a long-term overall strategy based on the insight into the relevance of the fundamental values (→ ch.3) to economic and social reason. The responsibility of an institution's managers includes all four areas of the determination, implementation, enforcement and development of ethical standards. One important aspect of this is found in the ethical standards for (international) personnel management (→ WITTMANN, Literature).

Women in trade: facts

- 64% of retail trade personnel in Switzerland (1995) are women.

- About 80% of the personnel of the World Shops of Fair Trade in Europe are women, who often work in an honorary capacity.
  (Fair Trade Yearbook 1997)

- Trade in capital: 58% of the micro-finance institutions for personal loans have a majority of women borrowers.
  (World Bank 1996, 11)

- 60% of the manpower in the informal sector in Africa, and 70% in agriculture, are women.
  (World Bank 2000, 20)

- According to the UNDP's Index of Human Development, the countries with the most pronounced gender empowerment measures (GEMs) are Norway among the OECD countries, Lithuania for Central/Eastern Europe, Botswana for Black Africa, Singapore for South East Asia, Hong Kong for East Asia, Sri Lanka for South Asia, the Bahamas for Latin America, and Tunisia for the Arab developing countries.
  (UNO/UNDP 2000, 211f.)

- The value of unpaid housework is estimated to be 30–50% of the gross national product – a value which has hardly ever appeared in the accounts of national economies, or not at all.
  (Madörin 1997)

- In the free-trade areas directly linked to world trade (Export Processing Zones), the proportion of women in the working population is about 70%.
  (UNO/UNIFEM 1994, 36)

Gender-specific aspects

World trade has gender-specific aspects as regards women both as agents in trade and as people affected by the negative effects of the rapid expansion of world trade. In industrial countries, the proportion of women in the retail trade has traditionally been high; it is now (slowly) increasing in management positions. The percentage of women Internet users is below average, while their proportion in initiatives of ethical trade is above average. In developing countries, their proportion in sectors that are partially adversely affected by world trade, such as agriculture and the informal sector, is very high; the same applies to growth industries such as micro-loans and micro-enterprises. Women's working conditions and pay in many sectors in developing countries are even worse than men's. In the fast-growing export zones linked to world trade, as well as in the other export-oriented sectors in developing countries, the percentage of women is very high.

Responsibility: empowerment of women = empowerment of ethics?

In terms of fundamental values, the equal treatment of women and men is a dictate of justice (→ ch. 3.2). Numerous studies also reveal that women in the economy tend to be more willing than men to include non-economic factors. In management positions, they are often more open towards ethics (→ ch. 5.2, reformers and idealists), and in situations characterized by poverty, they use resources more efficiently (e. g., repayment rate for personal loans, and higher productivity in subsistence agriculture and informal trade). Since to date, women have tended to be less integrated in power structures – although this is changing – they face the so-called factual constraints of such structures with less prejudice and more criticism, for instance with regard to participation in corrupt practices.

On the strength of these factors, the following proposition may be made: the empowerment of women tends to means the empowerment of ethics. Whether women labels are a means for the promotion of working conditions that are suitable for women is disputable. Moreover, justice with regard to gender also means justice between the genders. This may involve specific programmes for men, for instance by means of gender-specific training in business ethics.

The world's 25 biggest transnational corporations, according to foreign assets

Pos.	Corporation	Country	Foreign assets	Total assets
1	General Electric	USA	97.4	304.0
2	Ford Motor	USA	72.5	275.4
3	Royal Dutch/Shell	Netherlands/UK	70.0	115.0
4	General Motors	USA	0.0	228.9
5	Exxon	USA	54.6	96.1
6	Toyota	Japan	41.8	105.0
7	IBM	USA	39.9	81.5
8	Volkswagen	Germany	...	57.0
9	Nestlé	Switzerland	31.6	37.7
10	Daimler-Benz	Germany	30.9	76.2
11	Mobil	USA	30.4	43.6
12	FIAT	Italy	30.0	69.1
13	Hoechst	Germany	29.0	34.0
14	ABB	Switzerland	...	29.8
15	Bayer	Germany	...	30.3
16	Elf Aquitaine	France	26.7	42.0
17	Nissan	Japan	26.5	57.6
18	Unilever	Netherlands/UK	25.6	30.8
19	Siemens	Germany	25.6	67.1
20	Roche Holding	Switzerland	...	37.6
21	Sony	Japan	...	48.2
22	Mitsubishi	Japan	21.9	67.1
23	Seagram	Canada	21.8	22.2
24	Honda Motor	Japan	21.5	36.5
25	BMW	Germany	20.3	31.8

Foreign assets in 1997, in billion US dollars   Source: UNCTAD 1999

Definition

Transnational corporations (TNCs) are big companies operating in several countries; their performance and realization processes simultaneously take place at home and abroad. The size and organization required to call a company a TNC is a bone of contention.

International companies produce goods or services in one country and sell them from there through international trade.

Significance: rapid process of concentration

The number of TNCs worldwide is estimated to be 40,000; the share of the biggest 500 in world trade, 70 %, and in foreign investment, 80 %. 40 % of world trade takes place inside companies. Of the 50 TNCs that are the financially most potent in the world, 13 are based in the USA, 25 in Europe, and 9 in Japan (1997). The are among the driving forces of economic globalization. Worldwide, corporate mergers have greatly increased since the mid-1990s (→ graph). Forecasts assume that in the future, every industry is likely to be dominated by only about ten global players (oligopolization).

Specific responsibility: ethical trendsetters?

TNCs' investment strategies are constituent elements of world trade and thus of the distribution of opportunities for life. Their share in the responsibility for fair distribution and for a reduction of the gap between rich and poor is correspondingly great. To combat the increasing restraints on competition through oligopolization, it is worth considering a global anti-trust authority which includes markets other than those of the EU and the USA. TNCs are particularly well placed to circumvent nationally imposed limits through international structures, or put them under pressure by threatening to move jobs elsewhere. Ethical trade on the world market therefore requires corresponding global regulation mechanisms (→ chs 4.14 – 16, 5.21 – 24). Another particular responsibility of TNCs is the respect for multiculturalness in global context. It is their specific opportunity that, on the basis of their financial potency, they could set trends for ethical standards, codes, sustainability standards, social and environmental reports, and model working conditions – which means that in the case of a merger, these ethical standards would also have to be adopted!

Retail trade – facts in Switzerland

- 19% of companies and 14% of the working population work in the retail trade. 64% are women (1995).

- The average number of employees per company in Switzerland is 12.6 in the secondary sector (1998), 8.2 in the tertiary service sector, and 6 in the retail trade. Corporate size has been declining a great deal in recent years. The corporate structure in Switzerland, like in the EU, is overwhelmingly characterized by small businesses (EU: 93 of all the companies have fewer than 10 employees, only 1.1% more than 50).

- Supermarket chains (with more than 50 outlets) occupy 18% of the aggregate shop floor, concentrating on foodstuffs, clothing, and radio/television.

- The market share of the two major Swiss retail chains, Migros (23.7%) and Coop (24.6%) in foodstuffs (1999) reveals the high degree of concentration. By way of comparison: in the UK, the market share of the ten biggest supermarket chains amounts to 64%, that of the biggest, Tesco, to 14% (1996).

The eight biggest trading companies in Europe

	Turnover Europe Milliarden Euro	Turnover, abroad (%) 1995	1999
Carrefour/Promodes	59.8	40	43
Metro	34.9	30	66
Rewe	32.5	15	17
Tesco	27.2	5	10
Auchan	25.6	20	36
Aldi	25.4	25	37
Edeka	24.0	–	–
Intermarché	23.3	20	–

Source: Rudolph 2000

Definitions

Retail trade is the sale of merchandise to private households on the trader's own account or on a third party's account (i.e., on a commission basis). *Supermarket chains* are retailers which predominantly sell foodstuffs and household goods in numerous large-scale self-service outlets both nationally and internationally. *Wholesale trade* is the sale of merchandise to purchasers other than private households on the trader's own account or on a third party's account (i.e., on a commission basis).

Specific responsibility: direct or through associations

The small business size provides the *retail trade* with an opportunity to implement ethical standards faster and in a way that is easier to monitor. However, administrative chores like ethical monitoring must be able to be delegated, and the costs for licence fees for labels must be low, in order to be sustained by small businesses. As individual businesses, retail companies may set trends locally and regionally, but hardly nationally and internationally. At that level, their influence through the politics of their associations (small business associations, chambers of commerce) is highly significant. These associations should increase their profile with regard to trade and business ethics. The high proportion of women in the retail trade makes justice in terms of gender important (→ ch. 5.2).

Owing to their market power, *supermarket chains* have a particular opportunity and responsibility to promote an ethically responsible production through corresponding direct purchases and to manage the supply chain from the raw materials to the end user, as well as promoting ethical consumer conduct through product labels, corporate codes, and other marketing measures.

On account of its key position between producers and retailers, the *wholesale trade* can constitute an important bridge for ethical business, for instance by persuading both sides to comply with and monitor social and ecological codes of conduct, which is something that so far has not been put to sufficiently good use.

Working population according to sectors and gender

in selected countries

Country	Agriculture		Industry		Services	
	Men[1]	Women[1]	Men[1]	Women[1]	Men[1]	Women[1]
Albania	22	27	45	45	34	28
Egypt	32	43	25	9	43	48
Bangladesh	54	78	11	8	34	11
Brazil	28	23	26	9	45	68
Cambodia	71	79	6	3	23	18
Chile	19	4	34	14	47	81
Costa Rica	27	6	26	17	46	76
El Salvador	38	7	25	21	37	72
Honduras	53	7	19	27	28	66
Indonesia	41	42	21	16	39	42
Kenya	19	20	23	9	58	71
Lithuania	23	18	33	20	44	62
Syria	23	54	28	8	49	38
Thailand	49	52	22	17	29	32
Vietnam	70	71	12	9	18	20
Zimbabwe	23	38	32	10	46	52
OECD						
Germany	3	3	46	19	51	79
UK	3	1	38	13	59	86
Mexico	30	13	24	19	46	68
Switzerland	4	1	39	12	57	87
USA	4	2	34	13	63	85

1   Men means the proportion of all the working men of a country who work in this sector. The same applies to women.

The figures represent the average of 1992–97. In comparison with 1980, the service sector is on the increase everywhere, albeit at different rates. Retailers are usually included in this sector.

Source: World Development Indicators 2000. Author's own layout

Definition

Small producers are producers, particularly in developing countries, who produce things for their own requirements, the local market, and in individual cases for export; they work in agriculture, crafts and services, with only a few hectares of land and almost without any loan capital. Small traders market their own products or those of small producers on the local market or as intermediaries for export. Small producers and traders often operate in the informal sector.

Significance: majority of the working population in the south

30–70% of the working population in developing countries still work in agriculture, though their number is falling. The share of the non-agricultural working population in Latin America is between 50–80% and experiencing an upward trend; about 40% are self-employed and work in micro-firms. The majority of the working population in developing countries are small producers and traders. They are a very important safeguard of food and development. The significance of the local market apart from the world market is often underestimated in the debate about globalization.

Specific responsibility: support in exports

Exports may constitute a vital additional income for small producers and traders apart from the local market. In order to be able to do business worldwide, they need support for quality improvement and monitoring, micro-loans, a certain stability of raw material prices, and (usually cooperative) marketing structures. This support is provided through fair trade (→ ch. 5.11) and development cooperation but is also a task of ethically responsible trade. This is done through the promotion of imports from small producers and through cooperation with fair trade and development cooperation. In this manner, the fundamental value of partnership (→ ch. 3.8) is applied to weaker trading partners, which promotes humane development. Without this promotion, labels and codes of conduct may further marginalize small producers and traders in comparison with financially more potent trading partners. Intermediaries must be subjected to particular checks with regard to fair pricing in the monitoring of labels and codes.

Employment in the formal and informal economies of selected Latin American countries

Share of the non-agricultural working population		Informal economy				Formal economy
		Total	Self-employed	Household-related services	Microfirms	Total
Argentina	1990	47.5	24.7	7.9	14.9	52.5
	1996	53.6	27.1	7.8	18.7	46.4
Bolivia	1990	56.9	37.3	6.4	12.8	43.1
	1996	63.1	37.7	5.5	19.9	36.9
Brazil	1990	52.0	21.0	7.7	23.3	48.0
	1996	59.3	23.8	9.5	26.0	40.7
Chile	1990	49.9	23.6	8.1	18.3	50.1
	1996	50.9	22.7	6.8	21.4	49.1
Colombia	1990	55.2	23.5	5.4	26.3	44.8
	1996	57.2	25.9	3.8	27.5	42.8
Costa Rica	1990	42.3	18.1	5.8	18.4	57.7
	1996	47.2	17.4	5.2	24.6	52.6
Ecuador	1990	51.2	32.5	5.6	13.0	48.8
	1996	52.9	31.8	5.9	15.2	47.2
Mexico	1990	55.5	30.4	5.6	19.5	44.6
	1996	60.2	32.5	5.4	22.3	39.8
Panama	1990	40.5	20.4	7.2	12.8	59.5
	1996	41.6	20.7	7.0	13.9	58.3
Paraguay	1990	61.4	21.2	10.7	29.4	38.6
	1996	67.9	26.9	10.0	31.0	31.1
Peru	1990	51.8	35.3	5.1	11.4	48.2
	1996	57.9	37.4	4.2	16.3	42.1
Uruguay	1990	36.3	19.3	6.0	11.0	63.7
	1996	37.9	21.3	6.3	10.3	62.1
Venezuela	1990	38.8	22.1	4.1	12.6	61.2
	1996	47.7	28.1	2.4	17.2	52.3

Source: ILO, Informa, Panorama Laboral 97 (Lima, 1997); © IAT 1999

8.4 in 10 new jobs created in Latin America between 1990 and 1994 were in the informal sector! In Africa, 60% of the urban working population work in the informal sector. In Peru's capital, Lima, the proportion of women in this sector is 80%, in Indonesia 65% (ILO, 1997).

Definition

The *informal sector* comprises that part of the production of goods and services which works with a low degree of organization, low productivity, as a household operation, without any loan assets, without any employment agreements and thus in circumvention of welfare state requirements, with little security, and as a subsistence operation (ILO 1993). The *grey economy*, which is distinct from the informal sector, comprises unlawful economic activities in circumvention of legal obligations, particularly as illicit work.

Significance: high proportion, low security

In many countries, particularly in the cities of the South, more than half the population work in the information sector (→ table on the left). However, the informal sector is also on the increase in the big cities of industrial and transitional countries. In these insecure working conditions, even small personal problems such as illness or economic problems like inflation can drive people back into poverty again.

Specific responsibility: part of the trading chain?

The low security of employees in the informal sector means more responsibility for family networks and government or charitable institutions. The avoidance of tax in the informal sector gravely weakens the scope of government action and, conversely, casts doubts on the (democratic) credibility of many countries. Since efforts to integrate the informal sector into the formal sector are hardly ever successful, the promotion of small business and an improvement of working conditions in the informal sector is now also supported by development cooperation. Many subcontractors of export-oriented companies operate in the informal sector. It is unethical for companies in the formal sector to resort to subcontractors from the information sector in order to cut their pay and avoid ancillary wage costs. Thus codes of conduct which cover the entire trading chain also imply a share in trade-ethical responsibility for the informal sector; i.e., for raising the particularly low pay and inadequate social security prevalent in this sector. Trade-ethical guidelines in the treatment of the informal sector as the "economy of outcasts" remain to be developed!

Ways of ethical shareholder responsibility

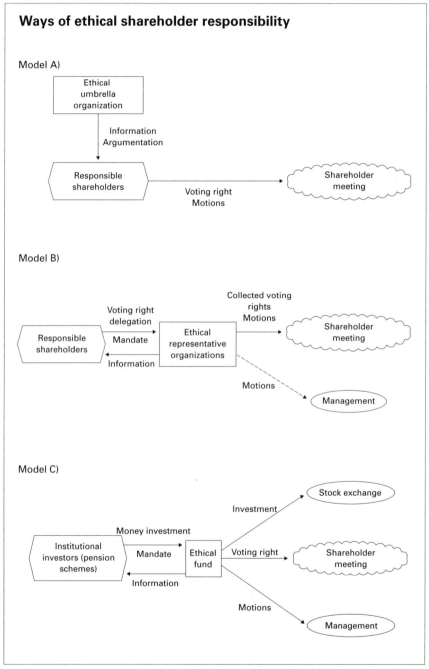

Model A)

Model B)

Model C)

© Stückelberger: Global Trade Ethics

Definitions

Shareholders are members of a joint-stock company who are entitled to dividends and the right to vote in shareholder meetings. *Shareholder value* denotes a joint-stock company's corporate policies to increase the shareholders' assets. Responsible shareholders (*l'actionnariat responsable, Aktionärsverantwortung*) observe the above-mentioned rights and obligations (legally, virtually none; ethically, the share in the responsibility for the company's ethical strategy and thus the corresponding monitoring of its management). In this manner, shareholders turn into careholders.

In Anglo-Saxon countries, *corporate governance* denotes a bundle of measures to ensure the working order and to monitor a company or institution, with which the shareholders or owners assume their overall responsibility and receive an appropriate compensation for their investment.

Direct and delegated shareholder responsibility

■ *Model A*

Shareholders' direct assumption of responsibility at the AGM, supported by social and ecological information from an umbrella organization or technical organization, such as the Interfaith Centre on Corporate Responsibility, New York, for religiously and ethically motivated shareholders.

■ *Model B*

The delegation of the right to vote to an ethics-based, specialized shareholder representative.

■ *Model C*

Institutional investors' investment in ethics funds, which in turn assume delegated shareholder responsibility in accordance with the fund criteria; the Ethos Foundation in Geneva is a case in point.

Specific responsibility: strengthen shareholders' obligations

An increasing number of specialized institutions support shareholders in the exercise of their responsibility, which must be welcome in ethical terms. Legislators must extend shareholders' obligations in order to strengthen the latter's responsibility in accordance with their power. The further rapid increase in the global concentration of power calls for globalized control mechanisms and for the creation of an institutional representation of social interest groups (*stakeholders*) in company's decision-making processes (joint-stock companies' AGMs).

5.9 Lobbyists 2: Employers' federations and chambers of commerce

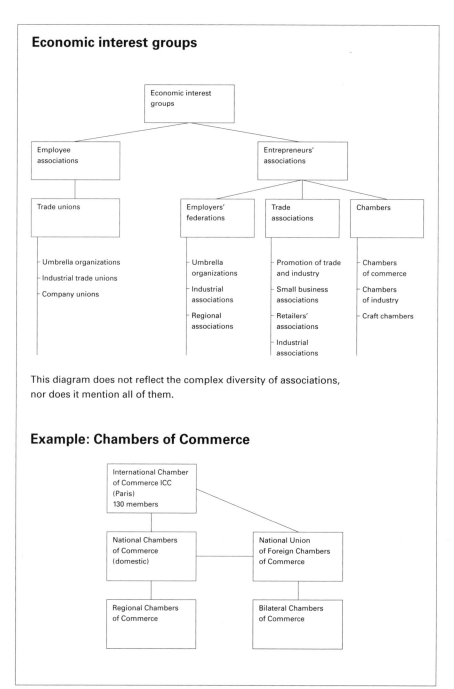

Economic interest groups

Economic interest groups

- Employee associations
  - Trade unions
    - Umbrella organizations
    - Industrial trade unions
    - Company unions
- Entrepreneurs' associations
  - Employers' federations
    - Umbrella organizations
    - Industrial associations
    - Regional associations
  - Trade associations
    - Promotion of trade and industry
    - Small business associations
    - Retailers' associations
    - Industrial associations
  - Chambers
    - Chambers of commerce
    - Chambers of industry
    - Craft chambers

This diagram does not reflect the complex diversity of associations, nor does it mention all of them.

Example: Chambers of Commerce

International Chamber of Commerce ICC (Paris) 130 members

National Chambers of Commerce (domestic)

National Union of Foreign Chambers of Commerce

Regional Chambers of Commerce

Bilateral Chambers of Commerce

Definition

Economic interest groups are associations which represent their members' economic interests in tariff negotiations with the government and society. Employees are represented by trade unions (→ ch. 5.10), employers by *employers' federations* – the classic triad of *employers' federations, industrial associations and chambers* of commerce, industry and trades) – and their umbrella organizations at regional, national and international levels.

Associations' instruments for ethical responsibility

- Training of members
- Provision of information about possible courses of action
- Awards and financial incentives for companies
- Promotion of coherence and shared standards, including rating, inside individual industries, among industries, and internationally
- Monitoring of one's own labels and codes, or participation in the monitoring of intersectoral labels and codes
- Sanctions against and blacklists of association members that fail to comply with ethical standards
- Consideration of ethical standards in national and multilateral lobbying with regard to trade policies
- Cooperation with NGOs

Specific responsibility: public welfare orientation

The ethical responsibility of economic interest groups means that they do not merely pursue their members' short-term interests such as cuts in social contributions and taxation on the employers' side (and wage rises on the employees' side) but include the long-term overall social responsibility for international social and ecological development. For an association, ethical conduct thus means to combine the legitimate representation of particular interests with public welfare orientation. In international trade, bilateral chambers of commerce (like the Sino-Swiss one) and the International Chamber of Commerce (ICC) can make important contributions to the partnership between trading partners and to voluntary and legal ethical standards.

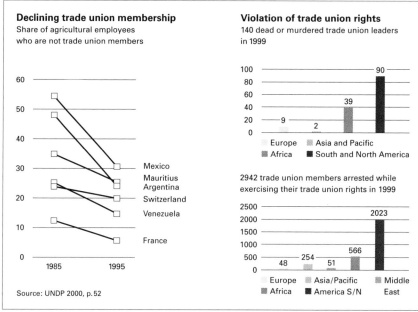

Declining trade union membership
Share of agricultural employees
who are not trade union members

Mexico
Mauritius
Argentina
Switzerland
Venezuela

France

1985   1995

Source: UNDP 2000, p. 52

Violation of trade union rights
140 dead or murdered trade union leaders
in 1999

100 — 90
80
60
40 — 39
20 — 9
2
0

Europe   Asia and Pacific
Africa   South and North America

2942 trade union members arrested while
exercising their trade union rights in 1999

2500
2000 — 2023
1500
1000
566
500 — 254
48   51
0

Europe   Asia/Pacific   Middle
Africa   America S/N   East

Growth in the number of international organizations 1909–1997

20000
18000
16000
14000
12000
10000
8000
6000
4000
2000
0

1909 56 60 64 68 76 81 86 90 91 92 93 94 95 95 95 96 97

1 Overall
2 INGOs

3 IGOs (b)
4 IGOs (a)

IGO: International Governmental Organization
INGO: International Non-Governmental Organization

1 Overall number of IGOs and INGOs
2 INGOs
3 IGOs (b): the number of IGOs that are tied to locations, persons and organizations and are not empowered under
international law, plus organization of special forms and internationally oriented national organizations
(Other International Bodies)
4 IGOs (a): the number of universal, intercontinental and regional IGOs empowered under international law
(Conventional International Bodies)

Source: *Globale Trends 2000*, p. 370

© Stückelberger: Global Trade Ethics

Definition

Trade unions are independent associations of employees under private law for the safeguard and implementation of their members' economic, social and cultural interests in their relations with employers, government and international authorities, and the general public.

Non-governmental organizations (NGOs) are independent associations under private law which usually specialize in a certain issue, try to increase the general public's sensitivity to it, provide aid, or participate in the creation of national and, particularly, international political processes and institutions.

The diversity and growing role of NGOs

NGOs are extremely heterogeneous and varied: small expert groups, broadly based charities, international environmental associations, international campaign networks of a given duration, militant action groups, etc. The focus is on policies regarding the environment, human rights, and development. NGOs work in international networks, which are increasing rapidly owing to the Internet. *De facto*, they are entities subject to international law although prevalent jurisprudence does not yet recognize them as such.

Specific responsibility: fair counterpower

International NGOs play an increasingly important role at international conferences and in their interaction with governments. Thus 1420 NGOs were registered at the 1992 UNCED Conference in Rio de Janeiro. What was said about economic organizations also applies to NGOs: the legitimate representation of particular interests must be combined with public welfare orientation. Trade unions and NGOs cannot and should not take over government tasks, but monitor them as a counterpower, and support them cooperatively as a partner wherever possible. The guarantee of trade unions' and NGOs' independence and freedom of action in relation with companies and government must be accorded particular protection on the basis of the fundamental values of freedom and fair participation.

Organizations of Fair Trade (FT)

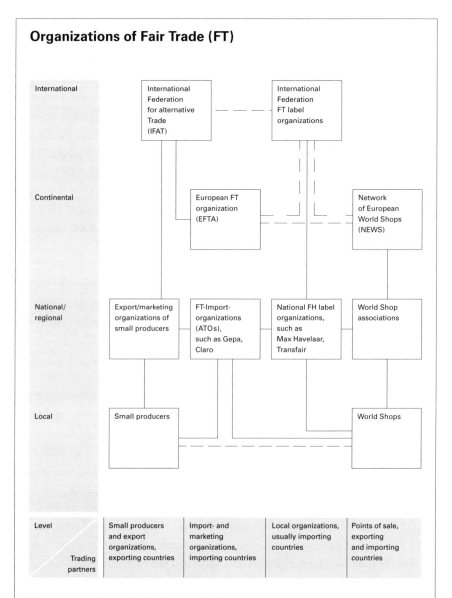

The **partners** of these fair trade organizations are
- the companies of the conventional economy which participate in fair trade (supermarkets, retail trade, processors),
- the bodies responsible for the above-mentioned organizations (charities, development-related organizations, partially companies).

© Stückelberger: Global Trade Ethics

Definition

Fair trade organizations promote fair trade, which is meant to open up markets for the economically disadvantaged – often small producers – and to improve their living and working conditions through fair prices and sustainable production (→ ch. 6.8).

Organizations of fair trade

- *Producers:* Small producers and their alliances in economically marginal regions all over the world, particularly in developing countries. The IFAT (*International Federation for Alternative Trade*), which was set up in 1989, consists of 88 producers' organizations from developing countries and 60 fair trade import organizations from industrial countries
- *Import organizations:* intermediaries (between small producers and world shops) and producer promoters, set up in the mid-1970s: ATO's (Alternative Trade Organizations, usually national), and EFTA (*European Fair Trade Association*) as the ATOs' umbrella organizations in Europe (examples: gepa in Germany, claro in Switzerland).
- *Label organizations:* Labelling and monitoring of individual products according to fair trade criteria, nationally under various names such as *Max Havelaar* or *Transfair*. The FLO (*Fairtrade Labelling Organizations International*) is the umbrella organization of the fair trade labelling organizations (14 from Europe and 1 each from the USA, Canada and Japan), established in 1997 (→ chs 5.14–5.16).
- *Sales outlets:* World shops since the early 1970s (the first in the Netherlands), later *retail trade* and *supermarkets*. NEWS (*Network of European World Shops*) has consisted of 15 national world shop associations in 13 countries, which represent 3000 shops, since 1994.

→ Appendix for the addresses of these organizations.

Specific responsibility: pioneering role

Fair trade conceives of itself as representing the interests of the poor in economically disadvantaged regions. In terms of trade ethics, it can play a pioneering role in the raising of standards in that it appeals to particularly sensitive consumers. For the promotion of small producers and the improvement of their quality standards, it remains dependent on development aid. One specific contribution is the partnership of those who buy from small producers.

Examples of church agents of ethical business

Type of structure / Level	Church management	Business ethical agencies	Educational institutions	Charities and action groups
International	World Council of Churches (WCC), World Confer. of Bishops, interfaith conferences	WCC offices at the UN, papal commission Justitia et Pax, Christian entrepreneurs	International ecumenical dialogues between churches and companies	Ecumenical Advocacy Alliance, involvement in codes, co-operation with companies
Continental	Continental councils of the bishops' conferences, and ecumenical church conferences	Agencies at continental and sub-continental church alliances	Continental associations of church education centres	Charity umbrella organizations at the EU (Aprodev, Cidse), trade campaigns
National/ regional	National Councils of Churches (public statements), interfaith debating circles	Institutes of business ethics, Justitia et Pax, Interfaith Centres for Corporate Responsibility	Theological faculties/ universities, academies and education centres, church media	Charities such as Brot für alle, Brot für die Welt, Christian Aid; fair trade projects
Local	Parishes, ministry, financial administration	Individual employees of the church	Religious and ethical education at all levels of education	World groups of develop-ment policy

→ Appendix for the homepages of some institutions.

Definition

Churches are Christian religious communities which comprise private individuals, local parishes, church federations at all levels, church works, institutions and initiative groups. *Religious communities* are collectives of people of the same faith in a wide variety of institutional forms; the terms often describes the world religions. *Charities* are non-profit-making institutions which support disadvantaged people with donations, information and legal aid, and which make efforts to have the disadvantages removed by improved general economic and political conditions.

Pioneers of responsible business

The importance of the Christian churches and the other religious communities for global business and sustainable development is recognized anew today. They used to shape the development of the economy in the historical past. It is not by accident that the Chairman of the Word Bank and the Archbishop of Canterbury have set up an interfaith consultation group. Churches and charities are often among the pioneers of responsible business and fair trade. Today, they increasingly work in global networks, also in cooperation with Buddhist, Hindu, Islamic and Jewish initiatives.

Specific responsibility: global ethics with spirituality

Responsible action is not only the result of ethical rules but needs to be rooted in a holistic world view. Religious roots mean responsibility towards God as the force that precedes and succeeds, newly creates, liberates, reconciles and guides human beings. Before and besides an ethical orientation, the religious communities' responsibility is therefore in preaching, worship, religious service and the communion from which responsibility for (global) welfare grows. This results in cooperation with economic agents and – where required – resistance against unfair trade. One specific challenge is active participation in a global ethos (Hans Küng is the pioneer) which stipulates shared values for the world economy on the basis of human rights, at the same time respects contextual value differences, and contributes towards the non-violent solution of value clashes.

Examples of networks for ethical economy

Level / Focus	Interdisciplinary "multi-stakeholder"	Company-oriented	Labour- and action-oriented	Research-oriented
International	International Society of Business, Economics and Ethics ISBEE	International Christian Union of Business Executives Uniapac	Third World Network TWN, Malaysia Jubilee 2000	International Association for Business and Society IABS
Continental	European Business Ethics Network EBEN Latin American Business Ethics Network LABEN	Corporate Social Responsibility Europe CSR	Europäische Soziale Bürgerbewegung Attac	
National	Deutsches Netzwerk Wirtschaftsethik DNWE Netzwerk für sozial verantwortliche Wirtschaft NSW (Switzerland)		Ethical Trading Initiative ETI (Germany)	Zentrum für Wirtschaftsethik ZfW (Konstanz, Germany) Institut für Wirtschaftsethik IWE (St. Gallen, CH)

These networks, too, make extensive use of electronic links.
→ Appendix for the addresses of their websites.

© Stückelberger: Global Trade Ethics

Definition

Networks for ethical business link agents from various sectors for the purpose of reinforcing the ethical and social responsibility of all those involved in the economy through the exchange of information, further education, research, comments and campaigns. They start from various premises and focus on different issues.

Boom since the 1990s

In parallel with the globalization drive, the number of business ethical networks has been rapidly growing since the 1990s and will soon be threatening to become a virtually impenetrable jungle (for examples, → table on the left). Originally, most of them had been launched by business ethicists (EBEN in 1989, ISBEE in 1992, IABS in 1990, with academics from over 100 countries). Today, companies themselves are playing an increasingly important role in these networks (e. g., CSR); they primarily link up by means of international conferences. In Europe, EBEN with members from 33 countries is the most important of these organizations, whose ancestors were the Christian employers' federations, such as Uniapac (1931) and Christian trade unions, as well as the Christian institutes for business and social ethics and the church/business discussion circles set up from the late 1960s (→ ch. 5.12).

Specific responsibility: involve Southern partners

The tripartite cooperation between governments, NGOs and private agents, which has already been realized in the ILO, points the way ahead for the solution of global business ethical problems, since no sector will be able to solve them on its own. Accordingly, the private networks mentioned here will increase in significance as partners in cooperation with multilateral institutions. The majority of these business ethical networks mainly consist of participants from Europe and North America. On the basis of the fundamental value of partnership, partners from transitional, threshold and development countries most be more strongly involved with their experiences and values, as ISBEE has so far done more than any others. Better interlinkage with label and code initiatives (→ ch. 4.5, 4.6) would improve efficiency even more.

129

Examples of private standardization institutions

ISO
International Organization for Standardization
Most important private standardization institution with 130 national standard associations. Standards: ISO 9000 ff: technical standards since 1987, ISO 14000 ff: environment management standards since 1996, ISO 21000: social standards (proposal of Brot für alle, not realized so far)

CENELEC
Comité Européen de Normalisation Electronique
Standardization in electric technology

ETSI
European Telecommunications Standards Institute
Standardization in telecommunications

ICC
International Chamber of Commerce
Standardization of the "International Commercial Terms"

FLO
Fair Trade Labelling Organizations International
Standardisation of fair trade labels worldwide (Max Havelaar, Transfair, etc.), focusing on Europe

SAI/CEPAA
Social Accountability International (up to 2000, CEPAA)
Accreditation institution for social standards with the SA 8000 series (Standard for Social Accountability, since 1997)

AA
Institute of Social and Ethical AccountAbility
AA1000 (AccountAbility Standard, since 1999)

IASC
International Accounting Standards Committee
Standardization of corporate accounting

FSC
Forest Stewardship Council
International standards for sustainable forestry; global FSC label

The WTO rules of the Agreement on Technical Barriers to Trade (TBT Agreement) make it incumbent on WTO member states to ensure that the private standardization organizations that are subject to central government control adopt the Code of Conduct for the Development, Adoption and Application of Standards (Appendix 3, TBT). Standards are understood as rules and guidelines for a product or production process, and compliance is not compulsory (App. 1).
→ Appendix for the addresses of these institutions.

© Stückelberger: Global Trade Ethics

Definition

Standardization is the process of the formulation of standards for products, processes or institutions by means of voluntary agreements or binding laws. *Standardization institutions* are private or government/supranational institutions which develop and adopt standards for certain target groups.

Trend towards harmonization/globalization of standards

Any institution of the legislative and judiciary institution is by definition an institution that can develop and implement standards! The private institutions can develop new series of standards without any complication, and in a free market, and they are growing in number at a corresponding rate. The rapid globalization forces us to harmonize the unmanageable diversity of technical (WTO: → ch. 5.22), legal, ecological and thus also ethical standards. The quest for a "world ethos" is expressive of this. In the past 20 years, there has been a development, first from technical to management-related standards and then to ecological, social and now integrated series of standards, which are often called ethical (→ Labels, ch. 4.5). One example of the latest tendencies in private standard harmonization is the Global Reporting Initiative (GRI). Launched by a wide variety of private and UN environment standardization institutions, and based in Boston, USA, it published globally applicable guidelines for organizations'/companies' reporting on sustainability in June 2000, and intends to introduce them from 2002.

Specific responsibility: check standards for ethics

Technical, legal, economic, social, ecological and moral standards (usually standardized measuring units or legal imperatives) developed by standardization institutions may be, but are not automatically, ethical standards that take their bearing from the fundamental values (→ chs 2.1, 3.0). They must be checked for their ethical substance individually, particularly by the most important technical committees. The search for a global ethos is necessary for world trade if any ethical hegemony should be prevented (→ chs 5.12, 5.24). The private global harmonization of standards may be a precursor of binding supranational regulations.

Process of the establishment and enforcement of standards

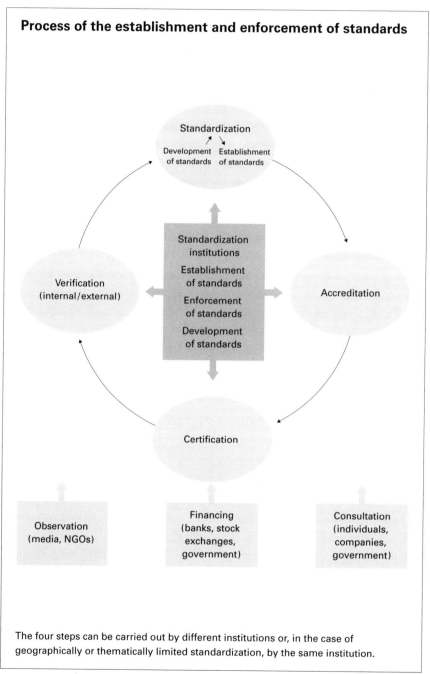

The four steps can be carried out by different institutions or, in the case of geographically or thematically limited standardization, by the same institution.

Definition

Accreditation is the process of granting a recognized certificate to an institution which has the competence and independence required by the methods it uses to check products, processes or institutions with regard to their compliance with a list of conduct criteria. This must be distinguished from checks on the standards themselves (certification, monitoring). *Accreditation institutions* are private or government/supranational institutions which are authorized to grant such accreditation. They are frequently identical with the standardization institution of a standard.

Example: standard SA8000

The graph on the left shows the institutions involved in the private, comprehensive social standard, Social Accountability 8000 (SA 8000), which was launched in 1997. It was developed by the Council on Economic Priorities (CEP) in New York and is now being implemented and further developed by Social Accountability International SAI (called Council on Economic Priorities Accreditation Agency CEPAA until 2000), New York. SAI has accredited five globally operating companies based in Europe and in the USA (as at August 2000): SGS, DNV, BVQI, ITS, UL (→ following chapter). Trade unions and NGOs are invited to apply for the status of certifier, but costs and criteria factually largely debar them. A company can only have individual production plants certified, which may undermine the standard. In addition, subcontractors are not covered by the standard.

Specific responsibility: selection of certifiers

Through the accreditation of certifiers, accreditation institutes make important decisions concerning the interpretation of standards and the seriousness of standard monitoring. In this respect, objectivity, independence, technical competence in the core areas of the standard series, representation of various social interest groups (stakeholders) in the decision-making bodies, also from developing countries, and costs that are capable of being sustained even by smaller and weaker companies, are important ethical criteria for the assessment of accreditation and certification institutions.

Example: Standard SA 8000

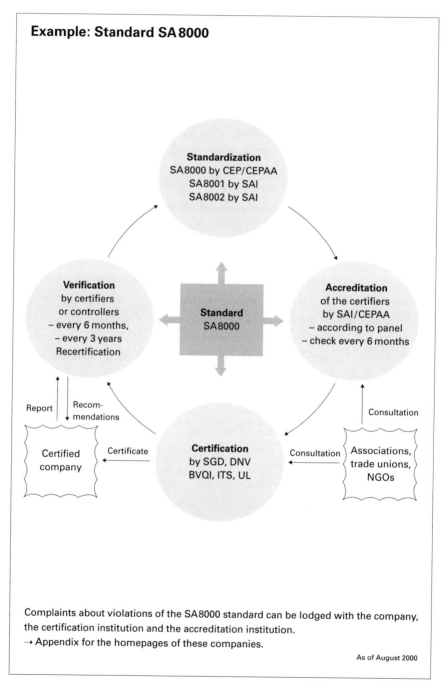

Complaints about violations of the SA8000 standard can be lodged with the company, the certification institution and the accreditation institution.
→ Appendix for the homepages of these companies.

As of August 2000

Definition

Certification is the process of granting a recognized certificate to an institution which has been monitored with regard to its compliance with a list of conduct criteria. *Certification institutions* are private or government/supranational institutions which are authorized to grant such certificates.

The certifiers' market

Multinational certification groups tend to certify international standards such as ISO and SA: for instance, SGS (Société Générale de Surveillance, Geneva, 1291 offices in 140 countries), BVQI (Bureau Veritas Quality International, London, 580 offices in 150 countries), DNV (Det Norske Veritas, Utrecht, 300 offices in 100 countries). The predominance of European and US certifiers and their fight for ethical certification reflects the world market (→ market of ethics, ch. 6.24). *Small companies* and NGOs predominantly certify national or product-specific standards but also international ones such as ISO. These are the environment offices, fair trade label organizations, associations, networks, and holders of labels and codes.

Specific responsibility: independence

What was said about accreditation institutions in the previous chapter also applies to certifiers. Particularly important are their credibility through competence and independence from certified companies, as well as fair participation (→ ch. 3.2); i.e., the fair involvement of the various participants (employer and employees) in the monitoring of firms/institutions. The fact that the five firms accredited for the certification of SA8000 (→ previous chapter) are themselves business partners of a wide variety of companies and are experienced in the technical domain rather than in social concerns and human rights has caused may local employee representatives to be mistrustful and to call for these firms' independence to be examined. Since certification costs are high for small businesses, certification in developing countries is often only possible in big export-oriented companies, which means that the award of certificates again reflects the North/South divide.

The world's five biggest auditing companies

PWC   *PricewaterhouseCoopers*
the world's biggest auditing and consulting company.
850 branches in 150 countries, headquarters in New York/USA.

AW   *Andersen Worldwide (Arthur Andersen)*
branches in 78 countries and cooperation agreements in 46 further
countries, headquarters in Chicago/USA since then. Fundamental
changes and crises ensued.

KPMG   *KPMG International*
KPMG International, 800 branches in 150 countries (the only one
of the five which is bigger in Europe than in the USA), headquarters
in Amstelveen/NL.

E&Y   *Ernst & Young International*
660 branches in 130 countries, headquarters in New York/USA.

DTT   *Deloitte Touche Tohamtsu*
Deloitte Touche Tohamtsu, branches in 130 countries, headquarters in
New York/USA.

(Figures 1999)

Annual turnover in billion US-Dollar

→ Appendix for the homepages of these companies.

© Stückelberger: Global Trade Ethics

The various forms of monitoring and controlling have already been described
(→ ch. 4.7). A more important role is played by NGOs with observation functions,
such as the „watch" organizations, Social Watch among them, the centres for business information like *Centre Info* in Switzerland and the *New Economics Foundation*
in the UK, and the charities. Here, the focus is on private *auditing companies*, which
are important agents of ethical trade.

Definition

Audits are an internal or external examination of processes in a company's or institution's production and finance. Auditing companies (auditors) are companies that
carry out external audits for the benefit of other companies' boards of directors.

Auditing firms: power concentration in the Big Five

The world's five biggest auditing companies (→ on the left) carry out the majority
of audits in international trade and for international organizations. This is increasingly supplemented by consultancy work – also in ethics (→ ch. 5.19) – that is also
offered by these firms. In 1977, they achieved 70 % of their turnover from auditing
work; today, the figure is 30 %. The share of consultancy work, partially with the
same customers, rose from 12 % to 50 %. This, coupled with the mega-mergers of
TNCs which are their clients, increasingly makes the auditors' independence
doubtful. The fall of Enron and Arthur Anderson in the US during 2002 shows a
deep crisis.

Specific responsibility: credibility

Credible auditing is of great ethical significance for fairness in trade, particularly
fair procedures, transparency and trust (cf. chs 3.3, 3.7, 3.9). This includes the auditors' responsibility for public welfare. The new *International Standard on Auditor
Independence* reveals that audit independence must be strengthened again, particularly among the Big Five. The costs of serious auditing are a development-ethical
problem for the smaller trading partners and also for development projects. Small
auditing firms in the South are often prone to corruption. Moreover, e-commerce
requires a new type of auditing.

Capital and insurance market

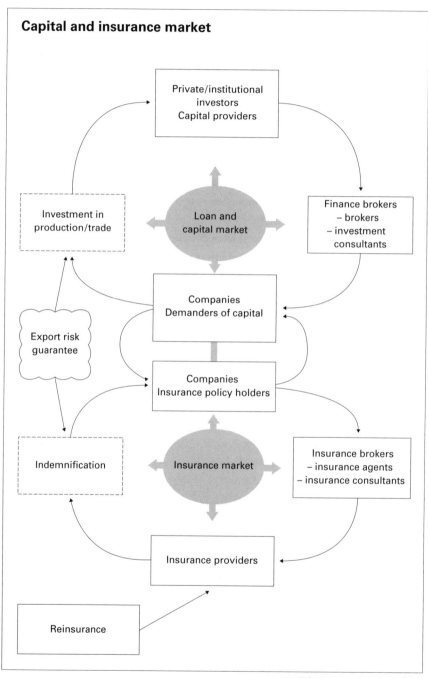

© Stückelberger: Global Trade Ethics

Definition

Ethically acting financing and insurance institutions are those which align all their activities with fundamental ethical values and which, in particular and to a substantial extent, grant loans, make investments and insure risks according to ethical criteria (→ ch. 6.14).

The agents of the financing and insurance business

Ethical demands are made on *exponents of the loan and capital market* such as

- private and institutional investors with regard to their investment criteria and their (global) investment policies;
- private-sector and public-sector banks with regard to their interest and debt policies (→ chs 6.4, 6.16), private banks with their forms of money transfer;
- finance brokers with regard to insider trading (→ ch. KOSLOWSKI 1997);
- prospective borrowers with regard to their investment policies.

Ethical demands are made on *exponents of the insurance market* such as

- insurers with regard to insurance policies for weaker trading partners and informal small traders (→ chs 5.6, 5.7);
- reinsurers with regard to uninsurable large-scale risks (e.g. environmental declaration of the insurance business with UNEP);
- insurance policy holders with regard to dishonest conduct (Moral Hazard).

Specific responsibility

Financing and insurance institutions are likely to have the greatest economic power and responsibility when it comes to the promotion of ethical standards in trade, for ethical business will only succeed in a free market if it can be financed and insured. The loan, capital and insurance markets possess various ethical aspects. The most important may well be the way in which they guide investment. No other industry is likely to be so strongly based on the trust between lender and borrower (→ Trust, ch. 3.9) as the finance industry. In the insurance business, compulsory insurance is an expression of the protection of victims and responsibility for the public welfare. It is in a tense relation with individual freedom. Ethical insurance clauses, such as are included in, say, government export risk guarantees, are part of insurance ethics.

Ethical advice

Company

- Corporate management
- Personnel management
- In-house ethics institutions

- Private ethics institutions
- Consultancy firms
- Ethics coaching
- Business Consultants
- Investment consultants
- Insurance consultants

Government

- Ethics commissions
  regional, national,
  international
- With a general brief or
  focused on specific issues

Agents
of ethical advice

Research and networks

- Ethics institutes
  at universities
- Ethics networks
- Standard institutions

**Churches/religious
communities**

- Individual pastoral care
- Religious services
- Discussion circles
- Ethics institutes

© Stückelberger: Global Trade Ethics

Definition
Ethics advisory institutions are private or public points of contact which advise individuals or collectives with regard to ethically responsible action (planning, implementation, monitoring) without making the actual decisions themselves.

Agents of business ethical advice
- In-house role played by the management, heads of departments and of personnel (→ management responsibility, ch. 5.2). Big companies have their own ethicists for training and advice. They must be expected to have had a well-founded theological or philosophical education in ethics.
- Explicit integration of ethics into the work done by business and investment consultants (ethical investment).
- Government ethics commissions (commissions that are relevant to trade exist for animal ethics, medical ethics and genetic technology, in particular) and ethicists in extra-parliamentary business advisory commissions.
- Consultancy agreements with university, church and private ethics institutes.
- Personal ministry and the coaching of people with management experience with regard to issues of professional ethics.
- Interdisciplinary and intercultural discussion circles about professional ethics, either in physical presence or virtually on the Internet.

Specific responsibility: no interest-induced bias
Any advisers are naturally tied to a wide variety of interests. Nevertheless, ethical advice must make an effort to represent no interests other than those of ethics;i.e.,to represent a moral clarification force outside economic and political interests. It is able to do so because it does not have to make the political and economic decisions itself. The guarantee of the independence of government ethics commissions, but particularly also of private-sector and in-house ethical advice, is therefore crucial to their credibility. The present boom in ethics is producing many self-appointed ethicists. Ethics, however, is a discipline like any other and requires the corresponding education and training.

Nation-states in world policy

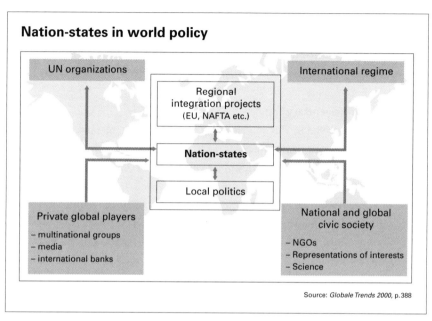

Source: *Globale Trends 2000*, p. 388

World order models

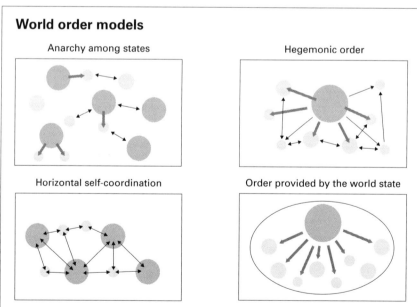

The present world order constitutes a mixture of ideal model types: Source: *Globale Trends 2000*, p. 381
the US hegemony with the UN's limited government character,
and coordination among nation-states through international organizations.

Definition

Nation-states are political entities with limited territories for the promotion and safeguard of human life through the (constitutional) rule and enforcement of law and the monopoly of power.

Nation-states and global governance

The view is gaining ground that nation states are losing their significance in a globalized world and are unable to solve the global problems. Factually, however, they remain the most important agents for creating the framework of political systems, either nationally, or internationally through treaties under international law and through their decisions in supranational or multilateral institutions. Formally, nation states set the WTO's course (informally, this is primarily done by blocks of countries and forces from the private sector). However, there are also ungovernable territories that give an impression of anarchy and have no de facto state power, for instance in Africa, where (illegal) trade is able to flourish. A variety of world order models (→ graph on the left) are now being discussed again under the heading of global governance.

Specific responsibility: equalization of interest

One main function of nation states is to balance interests both nationally and internationally; i.e., to solve the conflicts between fundamental values (→ ch. 3) by means of value judgments, with as little violence as possible, and through the democratic involvement of the population. In this manner, "politics in the service of basic needs" (EPPLER, 2000) would become politics in the service of the fundamental values. Today, nation states also have the task of reducing the lack of democracy in supranational and international institutions through the participation of national parliaments, for instance through the creation of a WTO parliament. Regardless of any international cooperation and coordination, however, nation states continue to be ethically obliged to make arrangements which go above and beyond the smallest common denominator of international obligations wherever they regard this as necessary for (trade) ethical reasons, for instance in the fields of trade and the environment.

Instruments of the common EU trade policy

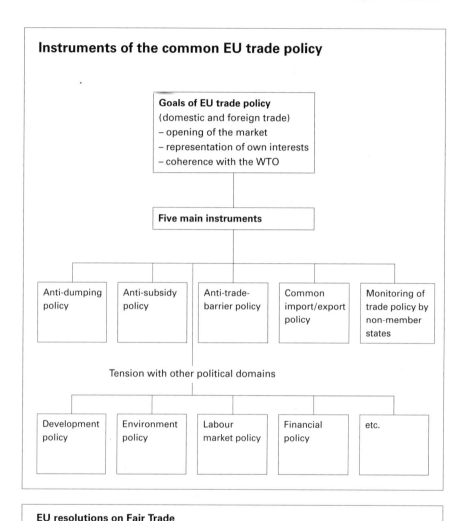

Goals of EU trade policy
(domestic and foreign trade)
– opening of the market
– representation of own interests
– coherence with the WTO

Five main instruments

| Anti-dumping policy | Anti-subsidy policy | Anti-trade-barrier policy | Common import/export policy | Monitoring of trade policy by non-member states |

Tension with other political domains

| Development policy | Environment policy | Labour market policy | Financial policy | etc. |

EU resolutions on Fair Trade

1994	EU parliament: resolution in favour of the "Promotion of Fairness and Solidarity in North/South Trade"
1996	Economic and Social Committee called on EU Commission to support Fair Trade
26. May 1998	EU parliament adopted Fassa Report on Fair Trade
2. July 1998	EU parliament: resolution of Fair Trade
29. November 1999	EU Commission: Report on Fair Trade addressed to the Council of Ministers

Definition

A supranational alliance of nations is authorized by its members to create and enforce certain rules and regulations. National regulations thus become community regulations, which overrides the former. A distinction must be made between such (economic) integration (EU) and an (economic) integration which wholly or largely does without any transfers of sovereignty rights (e.g., APEC, NAFTA, ECOWAS).

Fair EU trade policy?

The European Union (EU) is a great economic power which operates an effective foreign trade policy at community level ($\rightarrow$ graph on the left). With the euro, it is a world currency power. In terms of foreign and security policies, it is merely a regional power. The core of this foreign trade policy with regard to former colonies is the Lomé Convention with its combination of trade preferences and development aid, which, however, has been weakened under the pressure of WTO liberalization.

Specific responsibility: trade-ethical leadership

Inside the community/EU: Regional systems such as the EU are partially better placed to enforce ethical standards than multilateral institutions: they are more effective in imposing self-control on partner countries, with regard to possible sanctions when rules have been violated, and with regard to the transfer of resources for the improvement of weaker partner countries' trading opportunities. Thus the EU could assume an international role of leadership in relation to ethical business. The lack of democracy in supranational and international institutions results in an ethical legitimization problem of the rules they create; this gap can be filled by strengthening supranational parliaments.

Outside the community/globally: Whether regionalism will strengthen or weaken multilateralism remains to be seen. Regional integration must not make worldwide integration and solidarity more difficult. Domestic solidarity must not transmogrify into regional/continental group egotism. The promotion of fair trade by the EU (box) is positive. However, what should be aimed at is for ethical trade to shape EU trade policy in its entirety and not only in niches.

World Government

| Ministry of trade | Ministry of justice |
| Ministry of social services | Ministry of environment |

GATT Agreement, Article XX for "ethical" exemptions

Trade restrictions may be permitted in the following cases:

XX a) for the protection of public morals
     b) for the protection of life and health (people, animals, plants)
     c) with regard to the import/export of gold and silver
     d) to ensure coherence with other laws
     e) with regard to forced labour
     f) for the protection of national heritage (natural, archaeological, cultural)
     g) measures to preserve exhaustible natural resources
     h) with regard to the contract parties' other trade agreements
     i) to restrict exports of scarce goods
     j) if substantial, for the acquisition and distribution of products

These ethically justified exemptions (cf. Charnovitz 1998) may give fundamental values priority over the freedom of trade. However, Art. XX refers only to products of the same type. Ethically, though, separating products and their product processes cannot be justified.

Mandate, instruments, structure

The World Trade Organization (WTO) was set up in 1995, is based in Geneva, and has 140 member states at present. It is a special UN organization for the global management of international trade relations with the realization of free trade. Its main instruments are:

- GATT: rules for free trade in goods;
- GATS: rules for free trade in services;
- TRIPS: rules for the protection of intellectual property;
- TRIMS: rules for trade-related direct investment;
- combined with a monitoring and arbitration mechanism.

De iure, member states have one vote each irrespective of their size. *De facto*, policies are largely determined by the big economic blocks. Important are the numerous committees, for instance on development and on the environment. Today, the WTO has by far the greatest impact on world trade policy and has a more binding structure than other global issues (→ cartoon on the left).

Specific responsibility

The WTO roles are based on three fundamental principles: 1. equal treatment of all the contract parties (principle of most-favoured-nation treatment and non-discrimination), 2. equal treatment of one's own and other nations (national treatment), 3. freedom as regards the volume of traded goods (no import quotas, only customs tariffs are permitted). The implicit trade ethos that backs this up consists of the values of freedom and equal treatment. This means that justice (→ ch. 3.3) is realized in terms of equal treatment and procedures, but not in terms of performance, distribution and needs. Such a realization requires correspondingly strong mechanisms of other world organizations. Timid WTO approaches to strengthen weak trading partners, such as the poorest development countries, consist in transition periods and technical aid. These, however, are insufficient for a credible world trade ethics and require additional promises by the strong trading nations. Art. xx of the GATT offers ethical scope. The further development of humane world trade structures will have to involve proposals such as the democratization of WTO decisions (through a WTO parliament?), a world monopolies commission against restraints on competition through global mergers, and a world economic court.

Ratification of important conventions of the International Labour Organization

as at 4 April 2000

Principle	ILO Convention	Number of countries which have ratified it
Freedom of association and protection of the right to organize convention; Collective bargaining	Convention No. 87 (1948)	128
	Convention No. 98 (1949)	146
Minimum age	Convention No. 138 (1973)	88
Abolition of forced labour	Convention No. 29 (1930)	152
	Convention No. 105 (1957)	144
Equal remuneration discrimination (employment and occupation)	Convention No. 100 (1951)	145
	Convention No. 111 (1958)	142

Source: ILO 2000

ILO against child labour: faster and more binding

The ILO Convention No. 182 on the Worst Forms of Child Labour was unanimously adopted by the ILO's International Working Conference on 17 June 1999. It entered into force as an instrument of international law as early as 19 November 2000. It was ratified by fifty countries in this record time. Never before in the history of the ILO had a convention been ratified so quickly by so many member countries. In addition, countries which have not yet ratified the convention are also called upon to submit reports on their measures aimed at the elimination of the worst forms of child labour; these reports will be discussed by the ILO in 2002. Thus this ILO labour standard is quickly becoming more globally binding than previous standards.

Mandate, instruments, structure

The International Labour Organization (ILO) is based in Geneva, was established in 1919, and has 178 member states. Its mandate is to improve working conditions worldwide. For this purpose, it makes use of the following instruments (in order of their binding nature):

- *Declaration of 18 June 1998* about the eight ILO core labour standards: freedom of association, the right to organize, collective bargaining, abolition of forced labour, equality of opportunity and treatment, and other standards regulating conditions across the entire spectrum of work related issues. They are binding on all the member states whether they are ratified or not.
- *Conventions*, which must be ratified by member states (180 conventions).
- *Recommendations*, not binding (number: 185).
- *Codes of conduct resolutions and declarations*, not binding.
- *Monitoring mechanism* for conventions/recommendations.

The three main bodies are the International Labour Conference, which adopts conventions, etc., the Governing Body, and the International Labour Office. In its working conferences, the ILO has a tripartite decision-making structure of equivalent representatives of governments (2), employers (1) and employees (1).

Specific responsibility: enforcement of standards

The ILO's trade-ethical importance is in its tripartite and thus participative decision-making structure, and in its standards for humane and fair working conditions. However, the (sanction) instruments it has for their enforcement; i.e., its monitoring mechanism, is still too weak in comparison with, say, the WTO's arbitration mechanism. An ethical world trade which invokes the fundamental values of freedom, justice and sustainability (→ ch. 3) must enforce labour and environmental standards as consistently as it opens the markets. Only when this is done can any social and environmental clauses in trade agreements become effective (the WTO has delegated this issue to the ILO). The fact that the number of trade union members (→ ch. 5.10) is decreasing worldwide, however, raises the question as to whether the employers' participation in the tripartite structure will in future require additional forms of representation.

5.24 Global trade ethics under the conditions of a hegemonic power?

A hegemonic system is characterized by one single country claiming, and trying to establish, a position of leadership in relation to other countries; this claim is usually based on economic or military superiority. It may offer protection and integration, but its imbalance of power may also favour the abuse of power. Ever since World War II, and even more so since the disappearance of the bipolar world order in 1989, the rules of the world economy and thus also of world trade have essentially been shaped by the hegemonic power, the USA; indeed, rules often have been determined by its factual veto power, be it in multilateral institutions such as the IMF, the World Bank and the WTO, or be it through technological hegemony such as the Internet. Does the USA work as an ethical hegemonic power?

Apart from Europe, business ethics is particularly widespread in the USA. As we have seen, many private ethical standards and standardization institutions have their origin, and are based, in the US. However, this private business ethics is again and again in conflict with the US Congress blocking international government standards, for instance with regard to environmental conventions. The efforts for global standards and values, which are in line with the claim to hegemony, are ambivalent, too: in terms of a responsible world society, they are desirable, and the quest for a global ethos is necessary for world trade, yet ethical hegemony will have to be prevented, and cultural and ethical diversity will have to be respected, if we want a world society to emerge which is based on fundamental values such as freedom, justice, solidarity, sustainability and partnership (→ ch. 3). As a consequence of painful historical experiences with colonialism and missionary work, theological business ethics, in particular, wants a distinction to be made between culturally and contextually limited values and interculturally agreed ones in order to invalidate hegemonic claims.

6

Fields of action and tension

How are economic agents (→ ch. 5) able to translate into practice the fundamental values to which they feel committed (→ ch. 3) with the help of the various trade-ethical instruments (→ ch. 4)? What does this mean for pricing, time management, job policy, intercultural corporate strategy, and the way corruption is dealt with?

In this chapter, such applied fields of action will be depicted on the basis of *selected* examples. However, the fields of action are also fields of tension since the clashes of interests between participant groups again and again require a difficult value judgment, which may lead to ethical preference rules (→ ch. 2.4). Different ethical approaches deliberatively have been chosen for the 24 issues treated in this chapter so as to show that ethical reflection can be carried out in different ways. In any case, they can only be introductory stimuli to continue a given train of thought. A systematic step-by-step development of an ethical decision and the grounds for it (→ chs 2.2, 2.3) are beyond the scope of this introduction.

The ethical guidelines of the following applied fields of action are not fundamental values (criteria) that are independent of time and culture; rather, they are maxims that are valid in the context of a globalized market economy at the beginning of the 21st century (→ ch. 2.1). The objective is to hone our own judgment and conscience and those of institutions, to struggle for a responsible balance between economic, ecological, social, cultural and religious aspects of present-day business activities. Ready-to-use ethical recipes are rarely possible. However, this chapter will provide a few ethical conundrums.

Price components of Arabica coffee

Example: stock-exchange prices 2001, Contract C, ex-Dock New York

Exchange rate:	USD 1 = CHF 1.70
Max Havelaar minimum price:	USD 1.26/lb (454 g) raw Arabica coffee = CHF 4.72/kg
at a world market price of:	USD 0.75/lb (454 g) raw Arabica coffee = CHF 2.81/kg

Max Havelaar terms and conditions		Conventional terms and cond.		
	per kg in CHF		per kg in CHF	Diff.
– Max Havelaar small farmer	3.30	– Non-organized small farmer	1.69	49%
– Max-Havelaar cooperative (domestic transport, Investments)	1.42	– Intermediate trade (expenditure and profits)	1.12	100%
– **FOB price**	**4.72**		**2.81**	40%
– Maritime transport and insurance	0.25		0.25	
– **Costs, raw coffee, to port in Europe**	**4.97**		**3.06**	38%
– Customs and import duties	1.00		1.00	
– Roasting loss ≈ 15%	0.90		0.61	
– Roasting and packaging	2.90		2.90	
– Cost price	**9.76**		**7.57**	22%
– Trade: storage, distribution, advertising, taxes, margin	6.00		6.00	
– Max Havelaar license fee	0.33		0.00	
– **Final selling price, shop** (large-scale Swiss distributor)	**16.10**		**13.60**	16%

The example refers to February 2001, at the then prevailing average values and prices. World market prices and the dollar exchange rate have been changing rapidly, particularly since 1997. The average values may deviate from case to case. Max Havelaar's terms and conditions of trade also contain purchasing agreements – if possible, of one year's duration – and, at the producer's request, supply pre-financing facilities of up to 60% of the value of the ordered coffee volume.

Source: Max Havelaar Switzerland

Are market prices fair prices?

The price of a product is influenced by a great number of factors, particularly by the prices on the so-called factor markets – labour, real estate and capital goods such as pay, ground rents and interest rates – and by the prices on the goods markets. In trade, the margin defines the pricing scope. The trade margin is the difference between purchase or cost prices and the sales price of the goods sold by a trading operation; it serves to cover trading costs and to generate profits (→ ch. 6.7).

In a market economy, pricing is based on demand and supply, with varying price elasticity. Modern economics has largely banished the question as to the fairness of prices from positive theory and empiricism, and replaced it with the value of efficiency: a price serves the efficient distribution of scarce resources to the purposes desired by consumers. The market price as a balanced price derived from demand and supply is considered to be a fair price – at least in an ideal situation – because it includes a great number of individual assessments of the product by participants in the market (KOSLOWSKI, 1988). With this approach, the government would only have to intervene in the case of a market failure, i.e. a market that does not function sufficiently well. In a planned economy, however, central pricing is regarded as fair because it is supposed to make it easier to achieve fair distribution and to create a fair equilibrium between performance and needs.

Ten aspects of fair pricing

By way of example, we select justice from among the fundamental values (→ ch. 3) and ask the question as to what signposts its ten dimensions (→ ch. 3.2) can provide for pricing. The same could be done with the other fundamental values.

- *Performance-related justice*

  The production factors must be integrated into the price in such a manner that they provide as real a reflection as possible of the performance that went into the product. If product quality is taken into account in pricing, this is expressive of justice with regard to performance to the extent to which the performance that went into the product is – at least partially – reflected in its quality. Does it not contravene this justice, however, if, say, half the production costs of coffee consists of leasehold rents and interest on capital, whereas the work performed is paid so badly that you cannot live off it (→ ch. 6.2)? Justice with regard to performance also involves cost transparency, to which we will return in connection with ecological justice.

- *Needs-related justice*

  Equalization payments, social security contributions, taxes, etc., for the support of less well performing, poorer groups of people or of countries are a necessary part of production costs and have an impact on fair pricing. If such contributions are missing, the question must be asked as to whether the criterion of justice with regard to needs has been fulfilled.

- *Distributive justice*

  Market prices as prices balanced by demand and supply cannot ensure fair distribution on their own. Government instruments such as steering levies, the purchase of supply surpluses, price subsidies and taxes have a controlling character and are supposed to serve social equalization.

- *Justice as equal treatment*

  Fair prices also mean that producers receive the same price for the same performance regardless of their race, language, religion, gender, nationality or tribal membership.

- *Participatory justice*

  This may involve the producers' participation in pricing, the distribution of profits, and the control mechanisms.

- *Ecological justice*

  "Prices must tell the truth." This proposition about ecological Realpolitik by Ernst U. von Weizsäcker has become famous. Prices must reflect the truth of ecological and social costs; i.e., they must include the standards – largely recognized in terms of social ethics – of the causation and provision principles. According to E. U. von WEIZSÄCKER, the ecological costs included in today's prices only reflect between a fifth and a tenth of the entirety of environmental costs. A great deal of performance and its concomitant costs borne by the general public and, in particular, by nature, is not included in the costing of a product. The necessity of internalizing external costs to achieve cost transparency, which is recognized at least theoretically today, is an important part of the efforts made to attain justice with regard to performance and ecological justice, and it is a prerequisite for fair pricing.

- *Allocation-related justice*

  In a free economy, allocation is mainly carried out through prices. This is why in market-economic conditions, fair prices are the main instrument of fair allocation.

■ *Relational justice*
The fairness of prices must not only be measured in terms of their height or lowness at any given point in time, but also in terms of the stability, long-term outlook and reliability of pricing. These aspects favour fair relationships and are important for the fight against poverty, as the problems with strongly fluctuating raw material prices show, cocoa in the agricultural sector being a case in point.

■ *Procedural justice*
Fair prices are constitutionally controlled, legally realized (→ ch. 6.9, black market) and transparent, for instance without any hidden "useful incidental expenses", as bribes are euphemistically called.

■ *Interlinked justice*
The fundamental value of justice must be placed in relation to other fundamental values such as freedom or peace; i. e., the right measure must be struck between a price balanced by free demand and free supply, and a price that is informed by justice.

Fair trade (→ chs 5.11 and 6.8) operates with the logic of the market. It has proved that there may well be market segments for certain products even if they are sold at high extra charges. Fair prices declared in such a manner can also be a fair price in market terms. This price support need not result in the overproduction of this product if the extra charge is not invested in any increased production of this product but in the diversification into other product areas. "Fair trade carries out a kind of voluntary correction of market imperfections" (LIEBIG / SAUTTER, p. 124), as in the case of pay that safeguards people's existence, and it points in the direction of necessary corrections.

A fair price is not an absolute value but a process in the direction of improved justice.

How income is distributed

The shares in the overall income as owned by individual social strata

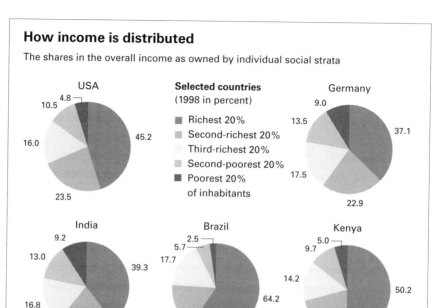

USA

4.8
10.5
45.2
16.0
23.5

Selected countries
(1998 in percent)

■ Richest 20%
▨ Second-richest 20%
□ Third-richest 20%
▨ Second-poorest 20%
■ Poorest 20%
of inhabitants

Germany

9.0
13.5
37.1
17.5
22.9

India

9.2
13.0
39.3
16.8
17.7
21.7

Brazil

2.5
5.7
17.7
64.2
17.7

Kenya

5.0
9.7
14.2
50.2
20.9

Source: Weltbank/UNDP

2000-18 epd-Entwicklungspolitik

The assets owned by B. Gates (Microsoft, USA) amount to 90 billion USD, the GNP of Singapore with its 3 million inhabitants is 95.4 billion USD. The assets of W. E. Buffet (investor, USA) amount to 28 billion USD, the GNP of Vietnam with its 78 million inhabitants is 28.8 billion USD (1999 figures). The assets owned by the world's three richest men now exceed the GNP of the poorest 48 countries.   Source: Forbes/World Bank

Social encyclical:

The refusal to pay the subsistence minimum amounts to violence.

"Let it be granted then that worker and employer may enter freely into agreements and, in particular, concerning the amount of the wage; yet there is always underlying such agreements an element of natural justice, and one greater and more ancient than the free consent of contracting parties, namely, that the wage shall not be less than enough to support a worker who is thrifty and upright. If, compelled by necessity or moved by fear of a worse evil, a worker accepts a harder condition, which although against his will he must accept because an employer or contractor imposes it, he certainly submits to force, against which justice cries out in protest."

Rerum novarum (1891), Encyclical Letter of Leo XIII on the Condition of the Working Classes (www.osjspm.org/cst/rn.htm).

Definition

Fair pay cannot be defined in general terms. However, it is possible for a lower limit to be fixed: the safeguard of the recipient's subsistence. In full-time employment, fair pay provides at least an income (paid out in money or, exceptionally, in kind) with which the employee is able to safeguard his or her own subsistence and that of his or her dependents who are unable to secure gainful employment ($\rightarrow$ Papal text on the left).

Subsistence minimum

What, then, is necessary to be able to subsist? We have found that the first fundamental value, the preservation of life ($\rightarrow$ ch. 3.1), depends on four dimensions: foodstuffs, clothing, housing; health; education, including access to information; and relationships and security. In many so-called low-pay countries, however, the minimum wages stipulated by an ILO Convention ($\rightarrow$ Literature) and/or prescribed by government is insufficient to safeguard subsistence or only sufficient as a living for the employee, who is unable to raize children on it, or does not leave any room for social relation, as is the case with 72-hour weeks such as are worked in Asian textile industries. Social security also includes the possibility of making minimum savings or being able to pay insurance premiums. However, pay often only safeguards subsistence if it is well above the legal minimum requirements.

Economic wage theory, and justice

Apart from safeguarding subsistence, the ten aspects of justice ($\rightarrow$ ch. 3.2) serve to assess economic wage theories, such as balanced wage, efficiency wage, and marginal productivity theory, in ethical terms. The fact that justice in its dimension of equal treatment means equal pay for equal work is self-evident. What is far more difficult to determine is the relative amount of pay that satisfies the demand of justice with regard to performance, and whether, from the point of view of fair distribution, a maximum wage should be fixed along with the minimum wage. In particular, the impact of wage policy on labour market policy and monetary policy should also be considered in terms of business ethics.

Necessary deceleration and acceleration

Acceleration or deceleration specifically adjusted to sectors is necessary.

Different rates of acceleration

Time management is now one of the most essential factors in world trade; it is also a major instrument used to influence transaction costs. New technologies such as IT and genetic technology are centrally characterized by the acceleration of exchange and breeding processes, respectively. Just-in-time delivery, e-commerce (→ ch. 4.10) and the deregulation of working and opening hours are also acceleration factors. Not only products, but also companies have an increasingly shorter life-cycle. Today, world companies last only an average of 20 years. However, acceleration takes place at greatly differing rates in the different world regions and social sectors, which results in considerable psychological, social, ecological and world political tensions.

Necessary acceleration

The accelerating demands for access of developing countries to the Internet, and for moratoria on genetic technology and for strategies of slowness (such as Slow Food instead of Fast Food) are leading to a situation whereby the rate of acceleration processes must be harmonized. The technological innovation rate must be better aligned with the slower biological and ecological processes of change. In specific sectors, it is necessary to decelerate.

Time management based on fundamental values

Ethically speaking, time management at the levels of logistics, technology, corporate strategy, culture, science and world politics must be based on fundamental values (→ ch. 3). Thus the fundamental value of "sustainability" raises the question as to how the tension between technological and biological rates of acceleration can be reduced. The fundamental values of "peace" and "justice" set the task of making time management socially and interculturally compatible, for instance by preventing the gap between the *information rich* (with their ever faster access to information) and the *information poor* from becoming explosive. Rates of change have to take into consideration the speed of the slowest participants.

6.4 Fair interest rates: The Reformer Calvin's rules

From interest ban to interest rules

Up to the Reformation:	Since the Reformation:
No interest, but... (interest ban, with exemptions)	**Interest permitted, but...** (interest allowed, with exemptions)

Calvin's seven rules on interest

(the rules printed on the following page as summarized by Christoph Stückelberger in today's idiom)

1 **Poor people should not be charged interest; they should be granted interest-free loans instead.**

2 **Money may be invested for profit, but money should also be given away as a donation.**

3 **The golden rule of mutuality must be observed.**

4 **The debtor should profit at least as much as the creditor.**

5 **Not the market, but Christian ethics, is the measure of justice.**

6 **The lending business should serve the common good.**

7 **A limitation of profit may be necessary; for instance, by means of a capital gains tax.**

Up to the time of the Reformation, interest was basically banned in Europe, not least because of the prohibition expounded in the Old Testament (Ex. 22:25; Deut. 23:20f). In terms of fact, however, it was badly eroded by many exemptions. The reputable Reformer in Geneva, John Calvin (1509–64), arrived at a basically favourable attitude towards the charging of interest, justifying his view by stating that the biblical ban's intention had been the protection of the poor. For Calvin, the service of one's neighbour also applied to the charging of interest, according to the 8th commandment, "Thou shalt not steal" (Ex. 20:15), and the golden rule "Therefore all things whatsoever ye would that men should do to you, do ye even so to them" (Matt. 7:12). This led him to the seven rules or exemptions with regard to interest:

"The first [exemption] is that poor people must not be charged any interest and that no one must be forced [to pay interest] if he is in a state of utter distress or has been afflicted by misfortune.

The second exemption is that no lender should be preoccupied with profit to such an extent as will make him fail to observe the necessary obligations nor that he, by investing his money safely, should disregard his poor brothers.

The third exemption is that nothing should be allowed to intervene [with an interest-bearing loan] that is not in harmony with natural equity and that if the matter is examined in accordance with Christ's rule, i.e., whatsoever ye would that men should do to you, etc., it shall be deemed generally valid.

The fourth exemption is that the borrower shall have as much or more profit from the borrowed money [than the lender].

Fifthly, that we neither judge what we may do [with regard to interest] in accordance with the general and traditional customs nor measure what is just and equitable against the world's injustice but that we derive our conduct from the word of God.

Sixthly, that we do not only consider the personal benefit of that which we have to deal with but also note what benefits the common weal. For it is manifest that the interest paid by the merchant constitutes a general payment (*pension publique*). Therefore it is well to ensure that the contract shall be more beneficial than detrimental to the common weal.

Seventhly, the measure be not exceeded which the laws of the region or town concede, although this does not always suffice, for they often allow whatever they are unable to alter or restrict by law. Thus preference must be given to equity, which shall curb that which is excessive."

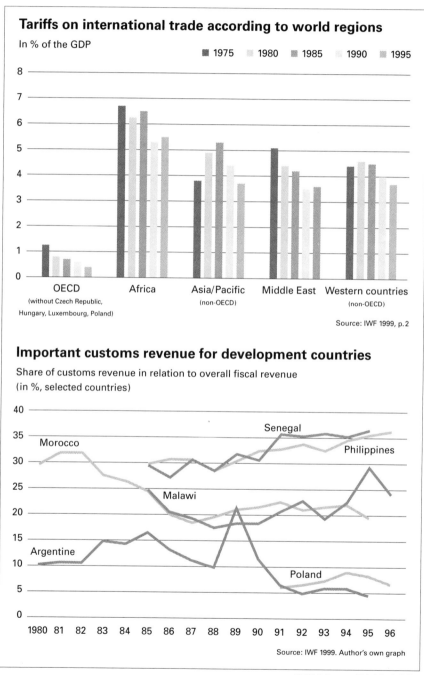

Tariffs on international trade according to world regions

In % of the GDP

■ 1975 ■ 1980 ■ 1985 ■ 1990 ■ 1995

OECD
(without Czech Republic,
Hungary, Luxembourg, Poland)

Africa

Asia/Pacific
(non-OECD)

Middle East

Western countries
(non-OECD)

Source: IWF 1999, p. 2

Important customs revenue for development countries

Share of customs revenue in relation to overall fiscal revenue
(in %, selected countries)

Senegal

Morocco

Philippines

Malawi

Argentine

Poland

1980 81 82 83 84 85 86 87 88 89 90 91 92 93 94 95 96

Source: IWF 1999. Author's own graph

© Stückelberger: Global Trade Ethics

Definition and types of tariff

Tariffs are government duties levied whenever goods cross the borders of a country or a customs area. Different types of tariff fulfil different functions: import, export and transit duties serve to control trade and to generate revenue. Protective, educational and prohibitive tariffs serve to reduce or control consumption (as with tobacco and alcohol). Preferential and retaliatory tariffs serve as positive and negative sanctions, respectively, with regard to other countries. A fair tariff system takes its bearings from the fundamental values (→ ch. 3).

An ethical assessment of the abolition of tariffs

The abolition of tariffs to reinforce world trade is a core element of the new world trade order which is stipulated by the GATT agreements and is to be implemented by the WTO. In terms of trade ethics, it has positive (+) and negative (−) implications:

- + A reduction in transaction costs, which is a core task of trade, strengthens trade, improves allocation, and cuts production prices. (This reduction is to an equal extent the result of cheaper means of communication and transport.)
- − The extension of cross-border trade with increased transport raises ecological costs, which must be covered by ecological control taxes (→ ch. 6.6) to internalize external costs.
- ± Competitive pressure is on the increase. This opens up new markets and accelerates structural adaptation and innovation, but also creates many "globalization victims".
- ± With the general reduction in tariffs, the preferential tariffs which, in terms of development policy, were important for developing countries' improved access to the markets of industrialized nations (→ ch. 4.16), have lost a great deal of their significance. Accordingly, there must be new measures for the promotion of those countries' trade.
- − In many developing countries, tariff revenue constitutes the biggest part of government income (→ opposite) since the remaining fiscal revenue amounts to very little owing to the population's poverty, the lack of infrastructure, corruption, tax evasion, exodus of capital, etc. For government budgets to stay in good health, a sound tax collection system must be established.

6.6 Fair taxation: Sharing public costs

Ethical principles for fiscal systems as exemplified by the fundamental value of justice

1	Performance	■ Principle of capability (taxed according to capability)
2	Needs	■ Use of taxes by an institution under public law
3	Distribution	■ Deductions and progression ■ Tax relief or subsidies
4	Equal treatment	■ Generality of taxation ■ Golden Rule[1]
5	Participation	■ Democratic determination of taxation and the control over it
6	Ecology	■ Environmental taxes ■ Taxes for global public goods[2]
7	Allocation	■ National tax harmonization ■ Global tax coordination[3]
8	Relationships	■ Rationally planned taxation ■ Practicability of taxation
9	Procedures	■ Fiscal transparency ■ Consistency ■ Punishment of tax fraud and tax evasion
10	Interlinked justice	■ Compliance with other fundamental values

1 "Support that fiscal system which you would choose if you did not know whether you were among the rich or among the poor." (Homburger, 1977, p. 233)
2 Global Public Goods, 1999, p. 109
3 Tanzi 1996

© Stückelberger: Global Trade Ethics

Definition

Taxes are payments of money which a polity, on the strength of its sovereignty, demands its economic subjects to pay to enable it to fulfil its communal tasks, without guaranteeing that individual taxpayers will receive a specific quid pro quo.

Function and types of taxation

The fair taxation of the various economic subjects is important in terms of business ethics and, at the same time, highly complex. Taxes have to fulfil two functions: the *fiscal purpose*, for the financing of government tasks by way of general expenses, and the *incentive purpose*, to avoid harmful conduct and to promote useful behaviour. The principle of neutrality requires that taxation should distort the market as little as possible, while at the same time, the government must make available the goods and protection mechanisms which would otherwise be lacking owing to market failure.

The various types of taxes have their own ethical relevance and problems ($\rightarrow$ table on the left): income taxes, consumption taxes/sales taxes, general property tax, corporate profit tax, capital gains tax, death duties and gift tax. Tax deduction systems must also take their bearings from the fundamental values.

Globally harmonized environment taxes?

Two aspects are particularly significant for globalized trade:
1. The question of tax harmonization; for instance, whether goods should be taxed in the country where they are purchased or in the country to which they are sold. The proposal of a "World Tax Organization" (TANZI 1996) is worth examining. Tanzi does not call for globally standardized taxes, but for the coordination of fiscal systems to reduce contradictions and blockages.
2. The fundamental value of sustainability demands a globally coordinated increase in ecological incentive taxes (taxes on energy consumption, transport, water consumption, use of land, and CO_2 output). Since a higher ecological efficiency has been proved to increase competitiveness ($\rightarrow$ STURM 1999), such incentive taxes are an additional allocation advantage for environmentally oriented trading companies.

Provision and distribution of profit

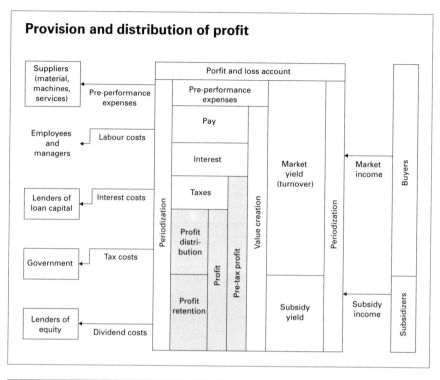

Four fundamental ethical questions regarding profit

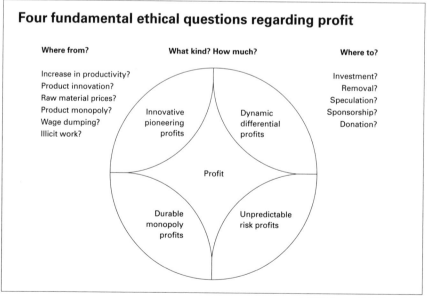

© Stückelberger: Global Trade Ethics

In the market mechanism of free competition between demand and supply, profit is a necessity for long-term economic activity in the private sector. As such, profit is neither good nor bad. However, four questions are ethically significant: How is profit made? What does it consist of? How high is it? What is it used for? The fairness of profit must be measured against the yardstick of whether the answers to these four questions respect the fundamental values (→ ch. 3).

Profit: where from?

Profits from, say, increases in productivity are positive if, for instance, they are made from innovation and increases in volume. It is ethically negative if increases in productivity result from low labour costs through illicit work or additional strains on the environment owing to longer transport distances (for profit before/after tax, → ch. 6.6).

Profit: what kind and how much?

Unpredictable risk profits (which are based on an uncertain future and serve as a protection against risk) and *innovative pioneering profits* (which serve as an incentive for innovative entrepreneurial courses of action) are also necessary for justice-oriented trade. *Dynamic differential profits* (which, for instance, result from the relocation of production factors into low-pay countries; i.e., from allocation decisions) are only fair if justice criteria such as pay that secures an existence or cost transparency with regard to transport are taken into consideration. *Permanent monopoly profits* are usually unfair because they are made at the expense of other trading entities, which may be equally efficient, and are not based on justice in terms of performance.

Of course, the ethically acceptable amount of profit cannot be determined in general terms. In the sense of an adequacy check (→ ch. 2.3), however, profits can be measured against the four questions, and profit policy can be corrected accordingly.

Profit: what for?

An ethical application of profits considers the aim of safeguarding economic activity in the long term and the various internal and external stakeholder groups, right down to donations to disadvantaged people as an expression of social responsibility. Justice in profit-making has priority over social mercifulness in profit distribution.

Fair trade reviews its criteria on the basis of its impact

Today's criteria	Future challenges
Fair (higher) price and partial prefinancing of production by purchasers	Danger of trading partners' alienation from the market. How can micro-producers be better prepared for world trade?
Direct purchase /elimination of intermediate trade	Intermediate trade is indispensable. How can it be fair, and are producers able to influence the trading relationship?
Disadvantages producers as the target group	How can industrial production be more integrated in fair trade along with the small producers?
Long-term trade relationships	Yes, but with the aim of producers' independence from fair trade.
Gender justice	How to take this into better consideration?
Consultation of producers and independent checks	How can product consultation be increased, and checks interlinked? Does self-financing entail fair trade having to concentrate on high-turnover products and producers?
Development through trade (as a supplement to aid)	Can and should fair trade be self-sufficient, i.e. finance itself completely through trade, or should the costs of product development, consultation and checks be supported with development monies in the long term?
Development-political education	What new approaches are necessary?
Exertion of influence on world trade policy	How can cooperation with other trade and the exertion of influence on world trade policy be increased?

Compiled and supplemented according to the self-critical analysis, "Entwicklungspolitische Wirkungen des Fairen Handels", 2000, pp. 273–301.

© Stückelberger: Global Trade Ethics

Definitions: one general, one specific

A distinction must be made between a broad and a narrow definition:

Fair trade in general is the organization of trade according to the fundamental values (listed in chapter 3), particularly justice, freedom, sustainability and peace; fair trade integrates the various dimensions of fairness (described in chapters 6.1–7).

Fair trade in particular (also *Fairer Handel* in German, *commerce équitable* in French) denotes trade as conducted by those trading agents (→ ch. 5.11) who are committed to the following aims and rules: "Fair trade aims at a more equitable distribution of revenues generated by international trade relations. The working and living conditions of producers and workers in the economically disadvantaged regions, particularly of the South, are supposed to be improved by providing the products offered by these producers and workers with market access at fair conditions. Fair trade activities promote sustainable development, which aims for social justice, economic development, the protection of the environment and the preservation of cultural diversity and which, if at all possible, strengthens trade in and between the countries of the South. The social and environmental standards aimed at by fair trade are in compliance with national law and the ILO Conventions and, wherever possible, transcend these. Fair trade is inspired by the active participation and shared responsibility of everyone involved in the trading chain. Continuous information activities are conducted to reinforce this consciousness… The credibility of fair trade is guaranteed by independent checks." (*Schweizer Forum Fairer Handel*, 2000, 2)

Significance and challenges

Fair trade has its roots in the first Third World Shops set up in the Netherlands in 1969. Today, there are more than 3000 World Shops and 70,000 points of sale for fair trade products in Europe alone (Central Europe, increasingly also in Southern Europe), with a retail turnover of 200–250 million euros (EU, 1999, 8). Fair trade is also spreading in the USA, Japan and in cities of developing countries.

Today, fair trade also sets itself self-critical challenges for further development (→ table on the left).

Grey economies

In % of the official GDP

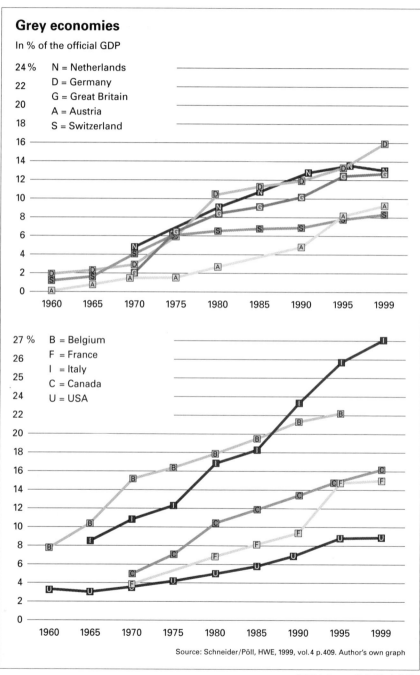

24 % N = Netherlands
22   D = Germany
20   G = Great Britain
      A = Austria
18   S = Switzerland

27 % B = Belgium
26   F = France
25   I = Italy
      C = Canada
24   U = USA

Source: Schneider/Pöll, HWE, 1999, vol. 4 p. 409. Author's own graph

© Stückelberger: Global Trade Ethics

Definition

Black-market trade denotes the illicit trade which caters a) to a demand which has a high purchasing power but is not satisfied, at prices that do not work on the regular markets, on account of an insufficient supply, and b) for an unsatisfied demand at comparably low prices that do not work on the regular markets on account of high levies and taxes. Black-market trade is part of the grey economy, of which illicit work is the biggest part (→ also chapter 5.7 on the informal sector).

Extent and causes

The *extent* of grey economies fluctuates, depending on how it is computed; however, all the methods used have registered an increase in the OECD countries between 1960 and 1997. According to the cash method, the grey economy increased from 11.2% to 15.04% of the GDP from 1985–1997 alone (→ table on the left). As far as the *causes* are concerned, surveys and calculations point to an increase in the tax burden, the regulation density, as well as a deterioration of fiscal morality. People's readiness to work in the grey economy has increased to a frightening degree.

Ethical assessment

Black-market trade can be understood as a sign of a badly and incompletely functioning market, of a lack of confidence in government, and of the mercilessness of the international competition for allocation advantages with low taxation. Nevertheless, black-market trade is still ethically unfair and harmful to the community because it *violates the criteria of fairness* (→ chs 6.1–8): prices that are unfair because they are not transparent; unfair pay, partially below the subsistence minimum, often with illicit work done by foreigners; unfair, sometimes usurious interest rates in black-market trade in capital; unfair profits resulting from excessively low production costs; evasion of customs duties (smuggling); i.e., unfair tariffs; evasion of levies, social insurance contributions and taxes (tax evasion), which jeopardizes the welfare state protection afforded to employers and the government's ability to fulfil its tasks; and violation of the fundamental value of trust, and of transparency.

Corruption according to economic sectors

Gallup International asked entrepreneurs in leading emerging countries: "In which sectors in your country is it highly probable, probable and improbable that senior civil servants take or give bribes?"
0 = very high degree of corruption; 10 = very low degree of corruption.

Construction and government tendering	1.5
Arms and defence industry	2.0
Energy (including oil)	3.5
Industry (including mining)	4.2
Health/social security	4.6
Telecommunications, postal services (equipment)	4.6
Civil aviation	5.0
Banking and financial services	5.3
Agriculture	6.0

Source: Transparency International 2000

Corporate reports on corruption; example: Shell

More and more firms have a corporate code which also prohibits corruption. Shell's annual report and homepage additionally carry the statistics of corruption cases disclosed in the firm (*Reported cases of bribery*):

Number of payments and value in US$	1997	1998	1999
Bribes directly or indirectly offered or paid by the company to third parties	0	0	0
Bribes directly or indirectly offered or paid to third parties by company employees	0	1 $300	1 $300
Bribes asked to be paid or paid by company employees	23 (small)	4 $75000	3 $153000

Source: Shell 2000

© Stückelberger: Global Trade Ethics

Definition and types of corruption

Corruption is the abuse of public or private power for private purposes aimed at gaining unjustified advantages of any kind. Corruption leads to the erosion of the common good through individual interests. Big-time corruption has its roots in a greed for power and riches, small-time corruption usually in impotence and poverty. The kind of corruption used to procure or accelerate the delivery of goods and services that are otherwise not available in the desired or legally obtainable period of time is particular to trade. The blurred zone between inadmissible corruption and nepotism/privileges/relational corruption can be described as grey corruption.

Corruption's adverse impact on the economy

The *consequences* of corruption, particularly of big-time but also of small-time corruption, include:

- *Misdirection of development (misallocation of resources)* in central sectors such as telecommunications, health, energy, transport systems and defence, in that investments are not made where they would be most necessary in economic, social and political terms while, say, public officials may expect to receive the biggest bribes.
- *Increased indebtedness*, in that investments in development do not produce the requisite economic benefits and thus aggravate payments of interest on debts and repayment of debts.
- *A lack of fiscal and other government revenues* for public tasks, owing to corrupt revenue officers and a correspondingly low payment morality.
- *Tax evasion*, in that monies obtained through corruption are not subject to taxation.
- *Reduction in quality*, for instance by non-fulfilment of standards, and in connection with this,
- *Increased security, health and environment risks* such as environmental disasters through accidents suffered by trading ships, negligent compliance with environmental regulations, circumvention of provisions regarding the sustainability of timber exploitation.
- *Distortion* of competition and the market.
- *Economic inefficiency*, in that, say, investment values are partly destroyed, and product prices are increased without a corresponding increase in performance.
- *Repellent effect on potential investors* and paralysis of a country's development spirit.

- *Increase in the wealth differential* (reinforcement of small elites, aggravation of the establishment of a middle class).
- Undermining of the acceptance of public and private *development cooperation.*
- *Increase in opaqueness,* leaving oneself prone to blackmail, and Mafia-like practices.
- *Loss of confidence* in the public and private sector.
- *Diminution of the moral integrity and credibility* of people and institutions.
- *Impairment of democracy* through rigged elections. Transparency is a prerequisite of democracy.
- *Gender dimension:* reinforcement of those who have power already (as a rule, the men); for instance, with regard to access to land, property, offices and positions of power.
- *Impairment of the legal system* and constitutional checks and balances until governments are simply incapable of governing.
- *Support of dictatorships* (which are apt to finance their private security bodies with bribes and thus become independent of control through their own parliaments) and armed rebel movements.

Why is corruption unethical?

Ethical criteria for the assessment of corruption include:

- *Justice:* Just is what reduces the gap between rich and poor. Just is what benefits poor people most (J. RAWLS). Big-time corruption increases the headway made by the powerful, thus widening the gap between rich and poor.
- *Equality, the same rights for everybody,* including the poor: bribery often perverts the rights of the poor, who do not have the means to give bribes or are not granted their rights by corrupt courts: "And thou shalt take no gift: for the gift blindeth the wize, and perverteth the words of the righteous." (Ex. 23:8)
- *Truth:* A recurring motivation for corruption is the fear of truth, which often also leads to a perversion of law and the constitutional state, and to violence. There is early evidence of this form of corruption in the Bible (in the story of Easter, Matt. 28:11-15).
- *Freedom:* Corruption creates an opaque web of mutual dependencies and leaves one prone to blackmail, thus precluding political freedom in the sense of the exercise of civil rights and duties of human rights.

- *Performance:* "Corruption replaces economic performance with theft" (thus the Peruvian Bishops' Conference in 1989). It distorts power because it does not reward performance but existing power.
- *Rationality/efficiency:* Corruption increases "efficiency" for individuals at the expense of the efficiency of the overall system, which is economically inefficient.
- *Participation:* Corruption is based on opaqueness, which is contradictory to democratic control and the participation of the general public. Participation in decision-making processes requires transparent information.
- *Human rights:* Corruption prevents individuals from being granted their lawful rights since they must buy these rights. Thus the "haves" are more likely to get their rights than the "have-nots". In 1998, the Eighth Assembly of the World Council of Churches described the protection of individuals from corruption as an elementary human right.
- *Sale of the unsaleable:* The sale of indulgences by a church is corruption because it makes people believe that salvation can be bought with money.
- *Common interest instead of self-interest:* Corruption places self-interest above the common interest. It is "the subversion of common interest by particular interests" (MAAK/ULRICH, 1999, 103).
- *Responsible exercise of power:* One frequent reason for corruption is short-term economic survival (the necessity of filling the order book). In bribery cases, it is often also greed for power or money that precludes any responsible exercise of power.

Access to information technologies

in selected countries   Data for 1998, per 1000 inhabitants

	Phone connections	Computers	Internet hosts
USA	640	406	113
Germany	550	255	18
Ukraine	186	5,6	0,4
Brazil	107	26	1,3
Thailand	80	20	0,3
Morocco	50	2,5	0,1
India	19	2,1	0,01
Industrialized countries	567	311	61
Dev. countries in East Asia	70	14	2,4
Sub-Sahara Africa	14	7,5	2,3

Source: World Bank, UNDP

People's Communication Charter (excerpt)

(Cultural Environment Movement CEM 1996)

Art. 1 All people are entitled to be treated with respect, according to the basic human rights standards of dignity, integrity, identity, and non-discrimination.

Art. 2 All people have the right of access to communication channels independent of governmental or commercial control.

Art. 3 In order to exercise their rights, people should have fair and equitable access to local and global resources and facilities for conventional and advanced channels of communication [...].

Art. 8 All people have the right to protect their cultural identity. This includes respect for people's pursuit of their cultural development and the right to free expression in languages they understand. [...]

Art. 12 All people have a right to universal access to and equitable use of cyberspace. Their rights to free and open communities in cyberspace, their freedom of electronic expression, and their freedom from electronic surveillance and intrusion, should be protected.

Source: CEM 1996

© Stückelberger: Global Trade Ethics

Information: a commodity

Information is, among other things, an economic commodity. It can be produced, traded in and consumed. In this sense, information has a value which results from its benefit and from the costs of production, procurement and transmission. However, this commodity has many particular features: information is immaterial, can be replicated in almost any number, is not used up on consumption, causes relatively little wear (except in cases of faulty transmission and the wear caused to any hardware), can be extended and condensed, is easy to transport but difficult to protect, has a tendency towards diffusion (once spread, it can hardly be recalled) and its value can be determined on the basis of its benefit.

Ethical aim: fair trade in information

At the same time, information is far more than a normal commodity. It contains numerous ethical aspects: journalists' professional ethos, media education, media law, media ecology, the dangers and risks of global networking, etc. (WIEGERLING 1998, NETHÖFEN 1999). Here, only four aspects relevant to trade ethics will be mentioned:

- *Information as a commodity, and the right to information:* Information is rightly traded as a profit-making commodity. However, it must not be subject to economic interests alone. In an information society, the right to information is a human right (→ People's Charter on the left).
- *The fair distribution of access to information* is therefore a focal ethical point. The still very unequal access to the Internet (→ table, ch. 4.10) and the globally concentrated media power, particularly in the USA and in Europe (→ table on the left) lead to the demand for a world communication system in a knowledge society which promotes fair access to information.
- *Benefit analysis on the basis of the fundamental values:* The benefit of (and damage caused by) the trade in and exchange of information must be measured against the fundamental values (→ ch. 3): does it promote justice, freedom, sustainability, peace, dignity, trust, etc.?
- *The instruments of ethical trade* (→ ch. 4) such as labels, company ratings, codes of conduct and the fairness criteria (→ chs 6.1–8) may also be applied to fair trade in information.

Price development of important raw materials, 1970–2000

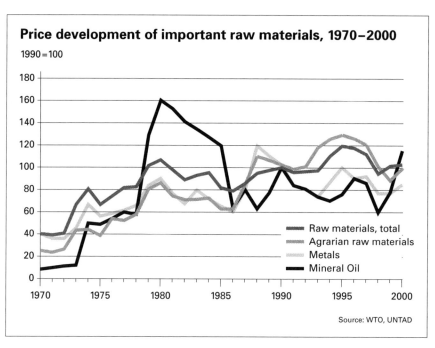

1990=100

Source: WTO, UNTAD

- Raw materials, total
- Agrarian raw materials
- Metals
- Mineral Oil

So much environmental space is taken up by a ton of copper

To produce a ton of copper, the following is required:

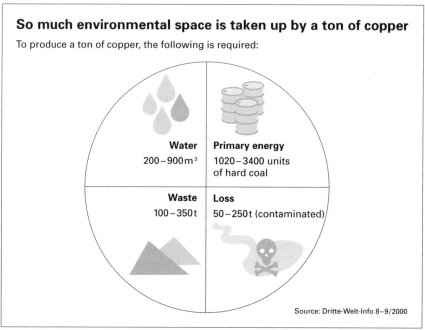

Water
200–900 m³

Primary energy
1020–3400 units
of hard coal

Waste
100–350 t

Loss
50–250 t (contaminated)

Source: Dritte-Welt-Info 8–9/2000

© Stückelberger: Global Trade Ethics

Definition: raw materials

Raw materials are unprocessed goods in *agriculture* (sugar, bananas, coffee, cocoa, tea, tobacco, wheat, corn, rice, wood, cotton, wool, india rubber, furs, cattle, jute, sisal), *minerals/metals* (copper, aluminium, tin, nickel, ores, lead, etc.), and *mineral oil*. *Raw material treaties* are goods agreements between producer and consumer countries with the aim of guaranteeing the sale of raw materials at appropriate and stable prices (at present for india rubber, coffee, cocoa, sugar and tin).

Facts and ethical challenges

- *Prices:* The low level and fluctuations of many raw material prices (→ graph on the left) are a direct cause of difficulties in development and the indebtedness of many developing countries (→ ch. 6.16), particularly in sub-Sahara Africa. Challenge with regard to justice: How can trade in raw materials make a stronger contribution towards price stabilization and raw material treaties?
- *Over-exploitation:* The mining of mineral raw materials causes gigantic damage to the environment today and uses up many resources (→ graph on the left). *Challenge with regard to sustainability:* How can the mining, processing and use of mineral and fossil raw materials become more efficient, and their consumption be reduced and recycled?
- *Indigenous peoples:* The British Minewatch organization estimates that, if present developments continue, 90 % of gold, 80 % of nickel, 60 % of copper, and half the coal will be mined in indigenous territories by 2010 (epd 2000, 3). *Challenge with regard to dignity/human rights:* How can the human rights of indigenous peoples be respected with codes of conduct, social clauses, agreements, campaigns and, if need be, trade boycotts (→ chs 4.6, 4.12 – 16)?
- *Raw material wars:* Very many current (civil) wars (→ ch. 6.21) are primarily battles for raw materials: Chechnya (gas, petroleum), Angola (gold, diamonds), Sierra Leone (gold, diamonds), Indonesia (gold, copper, nickel, silver, petroleum), Congo (various raw materials), Nigeria, Cameroons (petroleum), etc.
- *Challenge with regard to peace:* How can the national and international agents of raw material trade act responsibly in terms of policies that lead toward peace?

Ethical criteria for the assessment of genetic technology

(particularly with regard to non-human application)

Does genetic technology make a contribution towards the following issues
which could not be made by other technologies?

1. Reduction of hunger and poverty
2. Promotion of sustainability
3. Promotion of the fair distribution of natural resources,
   goods and services
4. Promotion of human and natural health
5. Promotion of security and social peace
6. Promotion of participation in decision-making
7. More efficient use of resources and funds in comparison with other technologies
   of comparable effect
8. Preservation of biological and cultural diversity
9. Adapted rate of development: harmonization of the technological, biological,
   political and ethical rates of development
10. Respect for the dignity of human and non-human beings

Biotechnology patents

Predominantly private owners

Ownership of patents on *bacillus thuringiensis*
according to owner groups, in %

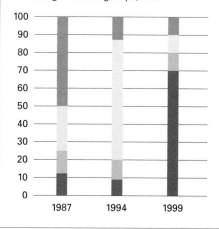

■ Universities and
public institutions

▨ Independent biotechnology firms
and private individuals

▨ Other organizations

■ The "Big 6"
(Dow, Novartis, Aventis, Monsanto,
Astra Zeneca, Du Pont)

Source: World Bank 2001, p.185

Society's judgment of the production of and trade in genetically modified organisms (GMOs) is highly controversial. A large ethical investment fund in Switzerland asked this author for *criteria for genetic technology for non-human application* (animals, plants). This is my proposal for seven criteria; a)–d) indicate variants of corporate conduct which may be used for over-weighting/under-weighting or as exclusion criteria for company ratings.

- *Sustainability.* Research into, production and release of GMOs: a) none (zero GMOs), b) unlimited, c) only small quota.[1]
- *Fair compensation.* Company's compensation for genetic resources within the framework of the Biodiversity Convention: a) company against, b) actively promoted in negotiations, c) compensations already paid.
- *Fair distribution.* Distribution of the ownership of agricultural land influenced by corporate products: a) increased concentration of land ownership, b) increase in the wider distribution of land ownership.
- *Participation.* Treatment of the obligation to declare GMOs: a) refusal, b) only if required by law, c) voluntary, even if not required by any law.[2]
- *Biodiversity.* Respect and promotion of biodiversity by the company: a) attempts to create a monopoly (e.g. terminator technology), b) support of farmers' rights and the possibility of continuing to grow traditional crops, c) training for farmers about the advantages and disadvantages of the various cultivation technologies.
- *Dignity of living things.* Production, use of or trade in transgenetic animals: a) none, b) within the provisions of the law, c) very restrictively, with the integrity of animals being respected (e.g., ability to reproduce, appearance), d) unlimited.
- *Demand-oriented research policy.* The company's focal points in genetic technology research take their bearings a) from the market potential alone (markets with high purchasing power), b) also from basic needs/fight against poverty, c) the company only trades and does not do any research.

---

1   Example: Guideline of Sustainable Asset Management (SAM), Zurich: "Companies which generate more than 5% of their turnover with products from genetically modified crops are excluded from SAM investment activities" (1998).

2   Example: SAM guideline: "Trading and distribution companies which do not make efforts to designate genetically modified foodstuffs as such for consumers are excluded from SAM investment activities" (1998).

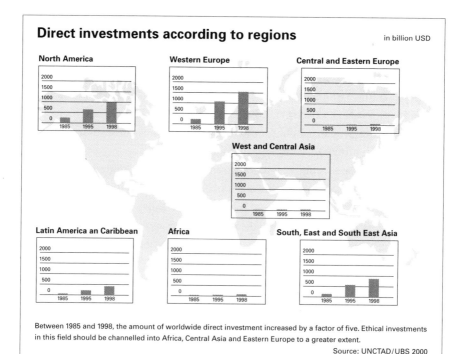

Direct investments according to regions

in billion USD

North America

Western Europe

Central and Eastern Europe

West and Central Asia

Latin America an Caribbean

Africa

South, East and South East Asia

Between 1985 and 1998, the amount of worldwide direct investment increased by a factor of five. Ethical investments in this field should be channelled into Africa, Central Asia and Eastern Europe to a greater extent.

Source: UNCTAD/UBS 2000

Ethical Investments

- **Exclusion criteria (negative catalogue)**
  Companies which operate in these areas are excluded for ethical reasons. As a rule: alcohol, tobacco, games of chance, nuclear power, armaments, and products from boycotted countries.

- **Quality criteria (positive catalogue)**
  Companies which fulfil such criteria either in absolute or relative terms (best-of-class approach) are included in ethical investments or over-weighted in mixed funds. Increasingly, the basic criterion is sustainability. The five dimensions of sustainability (→ ch. 3.4) can be applied.

- **Strict or integrated approach?**
  A strict approach includes in an investment portfolio only companies which satisfy the financial and ethical criteria. An integrated approach also includes companies which do not fulfil all the criteria completely satisfactorily, but conducts a rating with over-weighting or under-weighting of the companies and influences these by actively exercising its voting rights.

© Stückelberger: Global Trade Ethics

Trade has depended on functioning financial markets ever since the Middle Ages. It has often evolved in tandem with them. How can the credit and financial markets be aligned with the fundamental values?

Definition: ethical investments

Ethical investments are investments in the credit or capital market which, in addition to the classic investment criteria of yield, security and availability, also take into account social, ecological and development-political (positive/promoting or negative/excluding) criteria. The aim is investment in line with the fundamental values, availability and security of the capital, and an ethically acceptable optimal (not maximum) return.

Extend: billions, and still only a tenth of a per cent

In Switzerland, more than 5000 billion francs are in investments, of which 1450 billion are in shares. Ethical/ecological investments account for 5 billion francs, i.e. 0.01% (as at 2000). In the Anglo-Saxon world, ethical investments have the longest tradition, are most widespread and already represent several per cent of the sum-total of invested funds (EvB/WWF 2000).

Many types of possibilities of ethical investment

Banks and insurance companies (green, alternative, development-oriented, etc.), pension funds, bond issues/convertible bond issues, direct participation/venture capital, holding companies, joint-stock companies, ethical investment funds, investment clubs, real estate, foundations, donations and sponsorship.

A detailed list of Internet addresses of such ethical/ecological investments will be found in DEML/WEBER, 1999, pp. 256–265. For ethical assessment instruments, → ch. 4.11, Company ratings and stock-exchange indices.

Opportunities and limits

Today, ethical investments are an important incentive instrument of ethical business. Individual investments must be carefully checked for their criteria of varying strictness. Ethical investment will not make donations and sponsorship superfluous.

International currency transaction tax

Short-term financial speculation through currency transactions is supposed to be restrained through a tax in order to achieve a twofold effect, namely a reduction in the instability of the financial markets that is generated by such speculation, and the establishment of an international capital gains tax to contribute towards development financing. This idea, which was launched thirty years ago (Tobin 1972) is now gaining ever wider support (e.g. Spahn 1994, Wyplotz 1995, Schmidt 1999). Various solution models are summarized in simplified form below. An international agreement would determine the height of the tax, its mechanisms and right of application.

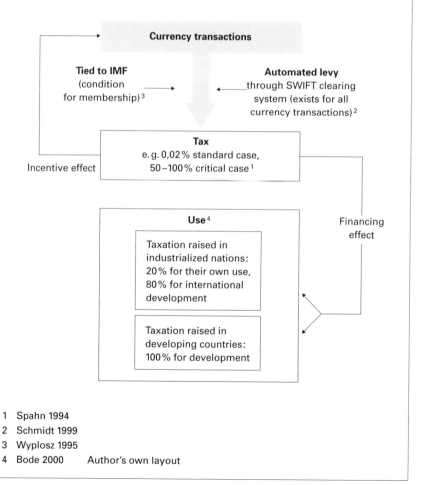

1   Spahn 1994
2   Schmidt 1999
3   Wyplosz 1995
4   Bode 2000   Author's own layout

© Stückelberger: Global Trade Ethics

Definition: foreign exchange trade and speculation

Foreign currency trade is the purchase and sale of foreign currency; i.e., of payment requests payable in foreign currencies from foreign locations. In the free market system, it primarily involves the currency transactions of interbank trade, but also of big multinational corporations. *Forward exchange deals* serve to cover the exchange rate risks. *Foreign exchange speculation* is the purchase/sale of foreign currencies in the expectation that their exchange rate will rise/fall and that they can be sold/repurchased at a profit.

Unimaginable volume

Short-term, speculative exchange deals shift some 1300 billion US dollars worldwide every day (1995)! This is many times the volume of real border-crossing trade in goods and services, which amounts to about 4800 billion US dollars *every year* and thus accounts for less than 2% of international capital movements.

Ethical challenge: civiliser l'argent

- Contentious proposition: "Capital market speculation is ethically admissible since it fulfils an objective function in the economy: it reduces the uncertainty about corporate shares' marketability on the stock exchange. Gains from speculation are therefore payments for that service." (KOSLOWSKI, 1997, 70)
- Short-term foreign exchange speculation must be "reined in" or "civilized" since its consequences in terms of trade policy (distortion of trade flows and allocation), national economies (destabilization of exchange rates) and development policy claim many victims, the high speculation profits do not satisfy the criteria of fair profit (→ ch. 6.7) and such speculation results in a massive increase in the inequality of ownership without making an essential contribution towards an improvement in living conditions (→ ch. 3.1).
- Various instruments of ethical business (→ ch. 4) are being discussed for foreign exchange trade and speculation, such as voluntary codes of conduct for agents on the spot and forward exchange markets, limitation of bonuses, and an international taxation of short-term currency transactions (→ left).

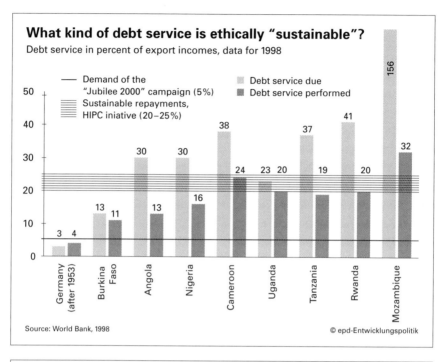

What kind of debt service is ethically "sustainable"?

Debt service in percent of export incomes, data for 1998

— Demand of the "Jubilee 2000" campaign (5%)
≡ Sustainable repayments, HIPC iniative (20–25%)
Debt service due
Debt service performed

Source: World Bank, 1998

© epd-Entwicklungspolitik

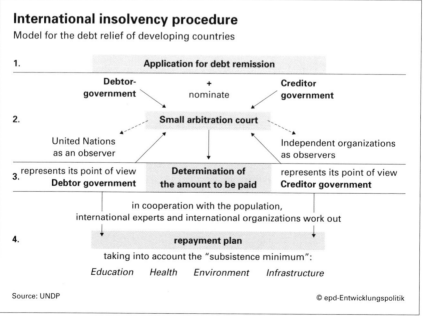

International insolvency procedure

Model for the debt relief of developing countries

1. **Application for debt remission**

Debtor-government + nominate Creditor government

2. **Small arbitration court**

United Nations as an observer   Independent organizations as observers

3. represents its point of view   **Determination of**   represents its point of view
   Debtor government   **the amount to be paid**   **Creditor government**

in cooperation with the population, international experts and international organizations work out

4. **repayment plan**

taking into account the "subsistence minimum":

Education   Health   Environment   Infrastructure

Source: UNDP

© epd-Entwicklungspolitik

© Stückelberger: Global Trade Ethics

Debt ethics: a central part of trade ethics

Debt ethics develops ethical criteria and possible problem solutions for dealing with the various form of private and public debt. Since the terms of trade play a crucial role with regard to the causes of indebtedness and its mastery, debt ethics are a central part of trade ethics.

Important approaches to debt relief

- *HIPC I and II:* initiatives by the IMF and the World Bank to cancel the debts of the poorest developing countries (Highly Indebted Poor Countries HIPC) down to a so-called sustainable debt burden of 25% of export revenues and with the condition of measures in the field of economic policy.
- *Jubilee 2000:* worldwide NGO/church campaign for the unconditional cancellation of HIPC countries' debts down to a sustainable debt burden of 5% of export revenues.
- *Creative debt relief with counterpart funds:* bilateral or multilateral debt relief, which uses part of the cancelled debt in local currency through a development fund for development projects in the country concerned. This has been successfully practised by Switzerland with twelve countries.
- *International insolvency law:* latterly called *Fair Transparent Arbitration Process* (FTAP), for highly indebted countries, with a participative decision-making mechanism between debtor and creditor countries.

Ethical criteria for debt relief measures

Debts must be cancelled in such a way that

- the remaining debt burden will respect safeguards of the population's existence (fundamental value: preservation of life);
- the causes of debt will be reduced (fundamental value: sustainability);
- both debtor and creditor will assume their share in the responsibility for the debt (fundamental value: power/responsibility);
- the debtors will profit more from the debt relief measures than the creditors (→ CALVIN, ch. 6.4, point 4);
- future generations will have only to take over a sustainable debt burden (fundamental value: [intergenerational] justice).

Figures mean people and fates

- The world's working population numbers about 3 billion. About a third have no fixed employment and live in poverty.

- The world's 200 biggest transnational corporations (TNCs) employ 18.8 million people worldwide. This is 0.6% of the world's working population. According to estimates, however, these companies account for more than 30% of world trade (available figures for the 500 biggest TNCs: they account for 70% of world trade).

- At the end of 2000, 160 million people were registered as unemployed, 50 million of them in industrial countries, including Central and Eastern Europe. Most of them are young and are looking for a job for the first time.

- Despite information technologies, a majority of the world population continues to work in agriculture.

- The information technologies have moved an estimated 12 million jobs from industrial nations to developing countries.

- The number of migrants and refugees who work outside their country of birth has increased from 75 million in 1965 to 120 million.

Sources: ILO 2001, Corporate Watch 2000, 3WI 2000

Overall value creation in the world in %

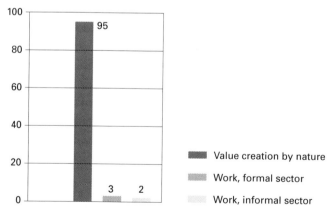

Source: Lang 1996

Effects of world trade on jobs

Positive effects:

- Economic growth serves to create jobs.
- Often better working conditions in export-oriented firms.
- Flexibility of gender-specific roles in the labour market.

Negative effects:

- "Jobless growth": growth without the creation of jobs.
- Accelerated outsourcing of jobs to other locations.
- Increase of migration and concomitant tensions.
- Increase of AIDS along trade routes and in trade centres.

Consequences of information technology for jobs

- High productivity and creation of new jobs owing to the rapid growth of information technology (IT).
- But IT also endangers jobs through automation and the reduction of mediation services ("disintermediation").
- Jobs' greater independence from places, resulting in different work organization, greater fluctuations, volatility.
- Gender-specific effects (e. g., more work done from home).
- Digital gap widens between rich and poor.
- Shift of data processing jobs from industrial countries to developing countries. (Source: ILO 2001)

Ethical challenge: relational mobility

The globalization of the world economy, crucially driven by world trade, demands increased mobility and flexibility from the working population. This leads to more migration and increases demands on long-term human partnerships and family structures. Job mobility results in and calls for relational mobility! Among the consequences of this are an increase in marriages where the partners live in different places for job reasons, divorces, migration conflicts, violence, as well as new forms of gender-specific role division and a digital gap even in the family itself. For these reasons, trade ethics must also take into account the social effects on relationships of the job mobility increased by world trade and promote relationship-friendly jobs.

Protection of human rights through private corporate codes

German development organizations and churches and representatives of the oil and gas industry have drawn up principles of conduct for that industry, particularly with regard to environmental and social matters. They include the following human rights concerns:

- *Land rights:* traditional land rights to be taken into account, resettlement only against compensation, recognition of indigenous cultures, negotiation rights.
- *Social/political human rights:* one human rights representative per company, combine legitimate corporate security with a reduction in violence.

Principles for the Code of Conduct within the Oil and Gas Industry, Stuttgart 2000

Implementation mechanisms
of the UN human rights conventions

Convention	Implementation body	Reporting	Appeals procedure (national)	Appeals procedure (individual)
International Pact on Economic, Social and Cultural Rights 1966	Social Committee	Yes		In preparation
International Pact on Civil and Political Rights 1966	Human Rights Committee	Yes	Optional	Optional
Convention against racial discrimination 1965	Committee against racial discrimination	Yes	Compulsory	Optional
Convention against the discrimination of women 1979	Convention against the discrimination of women	Yes		Optional
Convention against torture 1984	Convention against torture	Yes	Optional	Optional
Convention on the rights of children 1989	Committee for the rights of children	Yes		

© Stückelberger: Global Trade Ethics

Basic positions as regards trade and human rights

The debate about the determination of the relationship between trade and human rights is shaped by three basic positions:

- Trade and the protection of human rights must be kept apart. "Human rights is not the business of business." Trade is neither good nor bad and, per se, promotes freedom, openness, an exchange with the outside and, thus, indirectly human rights.
- Trade must respect human rights, and violations of human rights outside trade relations must be solved in separate political terms, not with the conditionality of trade policy.
- Trade and the protection of human rights are inextricably linked. Respect for human rights is a condition for normal trade relations and requires, for example, corresponding clauses in trade agreements.

Ethical value judgement

Seen from an ethical perspective, the protection of human rights cannot be invalidated or relativized since its basis, human dignity, is inalienable (→ ch. 3.7). Accordingly, trade in all its direct activities must respect human rights. However, it is a question of ethically weighing up by the most appropriate means whether trade relations are suitable to exercise pressure for human rights meant to be respected outside immediate trade activities. In this area, economic policy should strive for coherence between the various spheres of policy, particularly foreign, trade and human rights policy, even though it is well known that such coherence can never be fully achieved. In addition, different human rights often clash with each other, for instance the right of action and economic rights, or the right to development. In concrete cases of this nature, a value judgement (→ ch. 2.4) must be made as to which human right must be given primary protection and is a priority with regard to the protection of dignity. In principle, economic, social, cultural and religious rights are of equal value. For the protection of civic right, what is important is democratic participation in decision-making with regard to economic and trade policy and the structuring of an organization like the WTO (→ ch. 5.22) along these lines.

Source: Peter Spier, *Menschen*, 1981. Author's own layout

Definition: Intercultural management

Intercultural management (ICM) aims at a productive management of cultural diversity and at intercultural communication in business relations within companies, branches of international companies or between different trading companies in the private sector, as well as in the public sector and in NGOs. In addition, ICM also respects cultural values and diversity in the production of, trade in and consumption of goods and services. A central aspect of this is intercultural personnel management (→ ch. 6.20, interfaith).

Ethical challenge: diversity in unity

World trade requires an equilibrium between internationally agreed uniform fundamental values and standards (→ chs 3, 4.14, 5.14) and the respect for cultural diversity (→ ch. 3.7). Cultural diversity is not only a potential source of conflict but also something that enables the world to tackle its future (KRAMER/UNESCO 1998). In trade and investment policy (→ ch. 4.16), respect for cultural diversity is thus not only important for the protection of human rights but also for international stability and economic sustainability.

Trade makes a very great contribution towards the discovery of the wealth of cultures and towards intercultural communication in that it promotes certain cultural populations and marginalizes others; the rapid advance of the Internet (→ ch. 6.11, trade in information), for instance, is creating an Anglophone dominance. To satisfy the precept of fair prices, the societal and social external conflict costs arising from this must partially be included in production costs through social and cultural levies in the country of origin.

ICM is a deliberate management of interculturally conditioned value conflicts. The ethical training of a company's interculturally active personnel with regard to the company's own fundamental values is a prerequisite for and a first step towards encountering people from other value systems.

6.20 Trade and religions: Interfaith management

Interfaith Declaration of International Business Ethics

At the invitation of the Duke of Edinburgh, Prince Hassan of Jordan and Evelyn von Rothschild, Islamic, Jewish and Christian representatives of companies, banks, universities and religious institutions drew up the following declaration in 1994. It is a code of conduct for companies based on interfaith standards (excerpt):

These four principles – justice, love, stewardship, and honesty – form the moral basis of the Declaration that follows.

The Declaration

[...]

A) Business and Political Economy
All business activity takes place within the context of a political and economic system. It is recognized that:
1. Business is part of the social order. [...]
2. Competition between businesses has generally been shown to be the most effective way to ensure that resources are not wasted, costs are minimized, and prices fair. [...]
5. Because the free market system like any other is open to absue, it can be used for selfish or sectional interests, or it can be used for good. The State has an obligation to provide a framework of law in which business can operate honestly and fairly, and business will obey and respect the law of the State in which it operates. [...]
6. As business is a partnership of people of varying gifts, they should never be considered as merely a factor of production. [...]
8. Business has a responsibility to future generations.

B) The policies of a Business
[...]
3. The basis of the relationship with the principal stakeholders shall be honesty and fairness [particularly with the following stakeholders: employees, providers of finance, customers, suppliers, the community and shareholders]. [...]

Source: Webley 1999, S.103–107. Eigene Übersetzung

Definition: interfaith management

Interfaith management (IFM) aims at a productive management of religious diversity and at interfaith communication in business relations within companies, branches of international companies or between different trading companies in the private sector, as well as in the public sector and in NGOs. In addition, ICM also respects religious values and diversity in the production of, trade in and consumption of goods and services. A central aspect is religion-conscious personnel management (→ ch. 6.19, intercultural).

Religions influence trade

So far, IFM has hardly even been an issue in business ethics, but in view of the normative impact of religions on trade and its development (→ ch. 1.6), more attention should be paid to it. The great international "trading tribes" – Anglo-Saxon, Chinese, Jewish, Indian, Japanese – have been most profoundly influenced by the fundamental values of their respective religions (KOTKIN 1996).

Religions as merchandise?

Religions have always also been marketed. On a market over-saturated with goods, a further wave of this expansion appears to be emerging in the 21st century (→ ch. 4.4, cult marketing). Importing and marketing foreign holidays (which are usually religious in origin) is logically consistent with globalization. Within only a few years, the American holiday of Halloween on 31 October has found its place in Switzerland, and the daily *Tages-Anzeiger* newspaper of 30 October 2000 reported on how Halloween made cash registers ring. The import of the Chinese New Year has been forecast. The merchandise itself becomes a cult. This results in the threat of religious and cultural values shrinking into one single value: economic growth/increase in turnover. Fundamental values, however, can only serve as true foundations if they are deeply anchored in religion and culture, and religious and cultural holidays make an important contribution towards this. Their import and export must therefore be very carefully checked for ethical implications. This is probably most fruitfully done in a dialogue between trade and the churches/religious communities concerned. The World Bank made a good start with its World Faiths Development Dialogue.

States experiencing at least one armed conflict 1990–1999

Source: Project Ploughshares 2000/Author's own layout

Suppliers of the international arms trade 1992–97
Market share in %

Source: International Institute for Strategic Studies, 1998

© Stückelberger: Global Trade Ethics

Trade may encourage or endanger peace

The fundamental value of peace ($\rightarrow$ ch. 3.5) is strongly supported, but also endangered, by trade, particularly by cross-border trade. The most important contribution of trade towards peace is likely to be the provision to people of vital goods and services, for need creates tension. However, such trade will promote peace only if it is combined with fair, equalizing distribution, for "peace and justice are bedfellows", as the biblical Psalmist knew (Ps. 85 : 11). Below, a few factors of trade that encourage or endanger peace in brief:

Trade that endangers peace

- Economic growth that increases gap between rich and poor
- Unemployment through job relocations
- Financial markets prone to crises owing to speculative capital trading ($\rightarrow$ ch. 6.15)
- Fight for raw materials, particularly mineral resources ($\rightarrow$ ch. 6.12)
- Cultural violence ($\rightarrow$ ch. 6.19)
- Arms trade ($\rightarrow$ table)
- "War" with computer viruses
- Black-market trade ($\rightarrow$ ch. 6.9)
- Corruption in trade ($\rightarrow$ ch. 6.10)

Trade that promotes peace

- Economic growth combined with the fight against poverty
- Creation of jobs through trade ($\rightarrow$ ch. 6.15)
- Capital trading in the service of productive investments ($\rightarrow$ ch. 6.15)
- Raw materials agreements, protection of indigenous peoples ($\rightarrow$ ch. 6.12)
- Cultural diversity ($\rightarrow$ ch. 6.19)
- Trade in civilian goods
- Information technologies
- Transparent trade
- Fair, transparent prices ($\rightarrow$ ch. 6.1)

Suggestion: peace compatibility test

Ethical trade that takes its bearings from the fundamental value of peace could introduce a peace compatibility test within the framework of a corporate strategy or national or multinational trade policy. Similar to environment compatibility tests and to the instruments of labels, codes of conduct, company ratings or peace clauses in trade agreements ($\rightarrow$ chs 4.5, 4.6, 4.11, 4.15), peace-promoting trade may be honoured and rewarded.

Intensive and extensive effects of ethical instruments

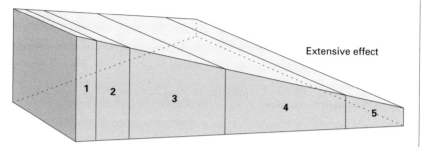

Extensive effect

1 2 3 4 5

Intensive effect

Instruments	Intensive effect	Extensive effect
Product label	Strong for the producers involved	Weak to medium: depending on the market share of the product
Corporate code	Strong for the company's scope of influence	Weak to medium: depending on the company's size
Company boycott	Strong: trigger instrument with public impact	Weak: only one company, only triggers measures
Stock-exchange	Weak to medium: only companies quoted on the stock-exchange	Strong: global signalling effect for many investors
National law	Medium to strong: depending on substance and scope	Medium: binding on all agents in one nation
International convention	Weak to medium: smallest common denominator	Strong: binding worldwide in signatory countries

© Stückelberger: Global Trade Ethics

Intensive and extensive effect

Segments 1–5 in the diagram on the left represent different instruments and agents of ethical business (→ chs 4 and 5). They have different intensive and extensive effects. Extensive denotes the extent of the company, products, countries, or market concerned. Intensive denotes the strictness of the ethical criteria, the intensity of the effect on individual producers, the environment, etc. Extensive and intensive effects should not be played off against each other but should both be recognized as necessary. Their difference, however, must be clearly reflected and transparently communicated to consumers and the general public.

Symbol or market power?

The first alternative jute-instead-of-plastic carrier bags of the early 1970s had a very strong symbolic content and triggered off lasting changes in thinking, yet had a very weak influence on the shopping bag market. Conversely, the new Dow Jones Sustainability Index is known only among investors but has a lasting influence on investment markets. Ethical business needs symbolical instruments by way of sign-posts, but also instruments which influence the markets – not only niches, but the actual mainstream. Ethical investment funds are very important as signposts but have so far accounted for less than 1% of worldwide capital investments. The remaining 99% are not unethical, per se, but must be equally justified in ethical terms.

Voluntary and legal measures

Voluntary and legal measures must also complement each other! Voluntary codes of conduct and labels can be implemented more quickly and often with stricter criteria than legal measures agreed by democratic decisions. They can and should supplement national and international regulations but cannot replace them since these can be made generally binding and practicable only through partnership, particularly with the South (UTTING 2000).

Thus, ethical business needs diverse, *multiple strategies* and instruments which complement each other.

6.23 Morals provide capital

Why ethics pay off

- Higher stability/lower corporate risks (security gain);
- lower interaction and friction costs; e.g., through strikes, crime, monitoring costs (productivity gain);
- higher productivity through the identification of personnel with the company and through lower fluctuation (motivation gain);
- strategy with a long-term basis (sustainability gain);
- higher consumption of ethically produced goods (turnover gain);
- advantages on the capital market with ratings (capital gain);
- wider acceptance among social stakeholder groups (image gain);
- in the long term, lower external costs (economic gain).

Long-term or also short-term?

Ethical business often pays off only in the long term. The aim of short-term profit maximization tends to lead people to disregard fundamental values. Even so, ethical business may also pay off in the short term if we think of security and motivation gains. The question as to whether ethics is profitable must also be supplemented by the question as to for whom ethics is profitable. For the company? For society? For future generations?

Fictitious ethics, instrumentalized ethics, value ethics

Corporate ethics turns into *fictitious ethics* if it does not go beyond verbal adaptation to an ethical glossary without inspiring any corresponding holistic changes in conduct. Equally great is the danger of *instrumentalized ethics*, where ethics are merely a means to the end of increasing profit and power; i. e. the fundamental values are instrumentalized to serve the aim of increasing one's power. The approach to business ethics advocated by this book is based on *fundamental values* and regards the compliance with and promotion of these fundamental values as the purpose of business. Economic action is therefore not an end in itself but has a function of service.

6.24 Conclusion: From market ethics to an ethics market

Ethical business in general and ethically acceptable trade in particular are continuing to gain ground and will probably do so for some time to come. There are three reasons for this:

1. the liberalization and globalization of markets, and the corresponding growth of trade that crosses borders, cultures and value systems;
2. the rapid worldwide dissemination of information about production and living conditions from all parts of the world by means of today's communication technologies; and
3. the increase in the significance of religions all over the world (in Europe, this process has been the slowest so far). The great number of approaches, agents and instruments of ethical business outlined in this book are evidence of this megatrend.

It is inherent in the system that these trends of setting the market ethical limits to provide it with guidance and protect it from crashes are accompanied by another trend whereby ethics itself turns into a market which is influenced by market forces. Market ethics thus turns into an ethics market. On the positive side, this results in a competition concerning ethical business which continues to launch new "products" of ethical business on the market. The diversity of labels, codes of conduct and ethical consultation services is expressive of this. On the negative side, it increases the danger of fictitious and instrumentalized ethics (→ ch. 6.23), cost increases through privatized certification systems and a proliferation of self-styled business ethicists.

And yet: let us use the opportunities presented by an ethically acceptable market and the ethics market. Let us hone our ability to distinguish between fictitious and sound ethics. Let us use market ethics as a supplement to, not as a replacement for, existing regulatory instruments, since those provide guiding limits (e. g., instruments of national legislation and of the equalization of the interests of social partnership). Let us seek cooperation and alliances with all those who are travelling along this route. This is the contribution that *Global Trade Ethics* seeks to make.

Appendix

Abbreviations

CE   A New Dictionary of Christian Ethics, London 1993 (4th ed.)
HCE   Handbuch der Christlichen Ethik, 3 Bde, Freiburg/Gütersloh, 1978
HWE   Handbuch der Wirtschaftsethik, 4 Bde, Gütersloh, 1999
LBE   Lexikon der Bioethik, 3 Bde, Gütersloh, 1998
LWE   Lexikon der Wirtschaftsethik, Freiburg/Basel/Vienna, 1993

Intergovernmental organizations
(numerous further abbreviations of organizations are listed with the Internet addresses)

ADB	Asian Development Bank
AfDB	African Development Bank
APEC	Asia-Pacific Economic Cooperation
ASEAN	Association of Southeast Asian Nations
ECOWAS	Economic Community of West African States
EU	European Union
GATS	General Agreement on Trade in Services
GATT	General Agreement on Tariffs and Trade
IDB	Inter-American Development Bank
IMF	International Monetary Fund
ILO	International Labour Organization
NAFTA	North American Free Trade Agreement
OECD	Organization for Economic Cooperation and Development
UNCTAD	United Nations Conference on Trade and Development
UNEP	United Nations Environmental Programme
UNDP	United Nations Development Programme
WB	World Bank
WTO	World Trade Organization

Sources and further literature

On Chapter 1: Basics I – Ethics in trade

1.1   *Ethics: Definition and scope*

HÖFFE, Otfried (ed.): *Lexikon der Ethik*, 3rd ed., Munich 1986.

RICH, Arthur, *Wirtschaftsethik*, vol. 1, Gütersloh 1984, pp. 15–41.

1.2   *Trade: Definition and scope*

MÜLLER-HAGEDORN, Lothar: *Der Handel*, Stuttgart 1988, pp. 13–63, 107–126.

AUSSCHUSS FÜR BEGRIFFSDEFINITIONEN AUS DER HANDELS- UND ABSATZWIRTSCHAFT (ed.): *Katalog E. Begriffsdefinitionen aus der Handels- und Absatzwirtschaft*, 4th ed., Cologne 1995, p. 28 ff.

1.3   *Trade: Institutions*

JAHRMANN, F.-Ulrich: *Aussenhandel*, Ludwigshafen 9th ed., 1998.

BRABECK-LETMATHE, Peter (Nestlé): *Konflikte zwischen Industrie und Handel. Gemeinsam ginge es besser*, Neue Zürcher Zeitung 14/11/2000, B 14.

1.4   *Levels of action for business ethics*

RICH, Arthur, *Wirtschaftsethik*, vol. 1, Gütersloh 1984, pp. 41–70.

ULRICH, Peter: *Integrative Wirtschaftsethik*, Berne 1998, pp. 289–463.

1.5   *Basic ethical questions in the goods exchange chain*

1.6   *The historical development of world trade and its ethics*

STIFTUNG ENTWICKLUNG UND FRIEDEN: *Globale Trends 2000*, Frankfurt/M. 1999.

RAMBOUSEK, Walter: *The Emergence of World Trade*, in: VOLKART, *The History of a World Trading Company*, Winterthur 1991, pp. 15–38.

SCHWEIZER, Peter: *Survivors in the Gold Coast. The Basel Missionaries in Colonial Ghana*, Accra 2000, p. 102.

WANNER, Gustaf A.: *Die Basler Handels-Gesellschaft A.G.*, Basel 1959.

KOTKIN, Joel: *Stämme der Macht. Der Erfolg weltweiter Clans in Wirtschaft und Politik*, Reinbek bei Hamburg 1996 (engl. Original: *"How Race, Religion and Identity Determine Success in the New Global Economy"*, New York 1992).

Various authors: *Interdependenzen von Religion und Wirtschaft*, HWE, vol. 1, pp. 567–780.

1.7   *Excursion: World trade in the Bible*

SEGBERS, Franz: *Die Herausforderung der Tora, Biblische Impulse für eine theologische Wirtschaftethik*, Luzern 2000.

1.8   *Globalization in business, politics and ethics*

WEIZSÄCKER, Christian von: *Logik der Globalisierung*, Göttingen 1999.

VAN DRIMMELEN, Rob: *Faith in a Global Economy*, Geneva 1998.

WORLD COUNCIL OF CHURCHES: *Globalizing Alternatives to Globalization*, Geneva 2000.

DICKINSON, Richard: *Economic Globalization: Deepening Challenge for Christians*, Geneva 1998.

DE SANTA ANA, Julio (ed.): *Sustainability and Globalization*, Geneva 1998.

LEUENBERGER, Theodor: *Weltethos und Weltwirtschaft,* Zeitschrift für Kulturaustausch ZfK 1993/1, pp. 67–70.

La mondialisation des anti-sociétés. Espaces rêvés et lieux communs, Cahiers de l'Institut Universitaire d'Etudes du Développement de Genève, Paris 1997.

KÜNG, Hans: *Weltethos für Weltpolitik und Weltwirtschaft,* Munich 1997, p. 218 ff.

FORNET-BETANCOURT, Raul (ed.): *Kapitalistische Globalisierung und Befreiung,* Frankfurt/M. 2000.

STÜCKELBERGER, Christoph: *Das Konzept der nachhaltigen Entwicklung um zwei Dimensionen erweitern. Ein Beitrag der Entwicklungsethik,* in: PETER, Hans-Balz (ed.), *Globalisierung, Ethik und Entwicklung,* Berne 1999, pp. 103–122.

1.9   *Definitions: Fair, sustainable, ethical, responsible trade*

INSTITUT UNIVERSITAIRE D'ETUDES DU DÉVELOPPEMENT (IUED): *Le commerce durable,* Geneva 2000.

On Chapter 2: Basics II – Methods of ethics

2.1   *From fundamental values to discretionary decisions*

RICH, Arthur: *Wirtschaftsethik,* vol. 1, Gütersloh 1984, pp. 169–241.

HONECKER, Martin: *Einführung in die Theologische Ethik,* Berlin 1990, pp. 211–234.

2.2   *Types of ethical grounds*

ULRICH, Peter: *Integrative Wirtschaftsethik,* Berne 1998, pp. 57–94.

WOLF, Jean-Claude / SCHABER, Peter: *Analytische Moralphilosophie,* Munich 1998.

RICH, Arthur: *Wirtschaftsethik,* vol. 1, Gütersloh 1984, pp. 24–41.

2.3   *The seven steps towards an ethical decision*

TÖDT, Heinz Eduard: *Perspektiven theologischer Ethik,* Munich 1988, pp. 21–84.

2.4   *Preference rules in value clashes*

RICH, Arthur: *Wirtschaftsethik,* vol. 2, Gütersloh 1990, pp. 36–40, 168–175.

STÜCKELBERGER, Christoph: *Umwelt und Entwicklung,* Stuttgart 1997, pp. 291–294, 299–305.

2.5   *Ethics and compromise*

STÜCKELBERGER, Christoph: *Vermittlung und Parteinahme. Der Versöhnungsauftrag der Kirchen in gesellschaftlichen Konflikten,* Zürich 1988, pp. 494–504.

2.6   *Ethics as a process*

2.7   *Factual constraints or decision-making options?*

RICH, Arthur: *Wirtschaftsethik,* vol. 1, Gütersloh 1984.

ULRICH, Peter: *Integrative Wirtschaftsethik,* Berne / Stuttgart 1998, pp. 131–165.

HUBER, Wolfgang: *Gerechtigkeit und Recht. Grundlinien christlicher Rechtsethik,* Gütersloh 1996, pp. 61–73: Verhältnis Recht und Ethik.

On Chapter 3: Fundamental values

3.1   Preservation of life

GOUDZWAARD, Bob/DE LANGE, Harry M.: *Weder Armut noch Überfluss. Plädoyer für eine neue Ökonomie*, Munich 1990.

MADELEY, John (ed., for the member Agencies of APRODEV): *Trade and the hungry. How International Trade Is Causing Hunger*, Brussels 1999.

3.2   Justice

RAWLS, John: *Eine Theorie der Gerechtigkeit*, Frankfurt 1979.

BEDFORD-STROHM, Heinrich: *Vorrang für die Armen. Auf dem Weg zu einer theologischen Theorie der Gerechtigkeit*, Gütersloh 1993.

HUBER, Wolfgang: *Gerechtigkeit und Recht*, Gütersloh 1996, 149–287.

STÜCKELBERGER, Christoph: *Welcher Handel ist fair?* Impulse 1/97, Berne 1997.

STÜCKELBERGER, Christoph: *Les valeurs fondamentales du commerce équitable et durable*, in: *IUED: Le commerce durable. Vers de plus justes pratiques commerciales entre le Nord et le Sud*, Geneva 2001, pp.75–95.

3.3   Freedom

HONECKER, Martin: *Einführung in die theologische Ethik*, Berlin 1990, pp.43–50.

STÜCKELBERGER, Christoph: *Umwelt und Entwicklung*, Stuttgart 1997, pp.305–310.

Europäische Evangelische Versammlung "Christliche Verantwortung für Europa", 24–30 March 1992, Schlussbericht Sektion V, epd-Dok. 17/1992, p. 29.

3.4   Sustainability

Unsere gemeinsame Zukunft. Der Brundtlandt-Bericht der Weltkommission für Umwelt und Entwicklung, Greven 1987, p. 46.

STÜCKELBERGER, Christoph: *Umwelt und Entwicklung*, Stuttgart 1997, pp. 263ff, 295ff.

STÜCKELBERGER, Christoph: *Das Konzept der nachhaltigen Entwicklung um zwei Dimensionen erweitern. Ein Beitrag der Entwicklungsethik*, in: PETER, Hans-Balz (ed.), *Globalisierung, Ethik und Entwicklung*, Berne 1999, pp.103–122.

3.5   Peace

SCHMIDT, Hans P.: *Schalom – die hebräisch-christliche Provokation*, in: *Weltfrieden und Revolution*, Frankfurt 1970, pp.131–167.

WEIZSÄCKER, Carl Friedrich von: *Die Zeit drängt*, Munich 1986, p.116.

3.6   Solidarity

Für eine Zukunft in Solidarität und Gerechtigkeit. Wort des Rates der Evangelischen Kirche in Deutschland und der deutschen Bischofskonferenz zur wirtschaftlichen und sozialen Lage in Deutschland, Bonn 1997.

NUSCHELER, Franz et al.: *Globale Solidarität. Die verschiedenen Kulturen und die Eine Welt*, Stuttgart 1997.

ROTTLÄNDER, Peter: *Die "Ressource Solidarität" als Basis für eine Begründung von Entwicklungszusammenarbeit*, in: PETER, Hans-Balz (ed.), *Globalisierung, Ethik und Entwicklung*, Berne/Stuttgart/Vienna 1999, pp.147–167.

3.7   Dignity

KANT, I.: *Grundlegung zur Metaphysik der Sitten, complete works*, vol. VII, Frankfurt 1968, BA 77.

HUBER, Wolfgang/TÖDT, Heinz Eduard: *Menschenrechte*, Stuttgart 1977, pp. 40 ff, 84 ff, 145 ff.

STÜCKELBERGER, Christoph: *Umwelt und Entwicklung*, Stuttgart 1997, pp. 263–273.

TAYLOR, Paul: *Respect for Nature*, Princeton 1986, p. 61ff.

TEUTSCH, Gotthard M.: *Würde der Kreatur. Eräuterungen zu einem neuen Verfassungs-begriff am Beispiel des Tieres*, Berne 1995.

BONDOLFI, Alberto et al. (eds.): *Würde der Kreatur. Essays zu einem kontroversen Thema*, Zürich 1997.

3.8   Partnership

RICH, Arthur: *Wirtschaftsethik*, vol. 1, Zürich 1984, pp. 196–201.

BIERVERT, Bernd/HELD, Martin (eds.): *Das Menschenbild der ökonomischen Theorie. Zur Natur des Menschen*, Frankfurt/M. 1991.

3.9   Trust

RIPPERGER, Tanja: *Vertrauen im institutionellen Rahmen*, HWE, vol. 3, pp. 67–99.

THOMMEN, Jean-Pierre: *Managementorientierte Betriebswirtschaftslehre*, Zürich, 5th ed., 1996, p. 790 f.

3.10   Power/reponsibility

KÜNG, Hans: *Weltethos für Weltpolitik und Weltwirtschaft*, Munich 1997, p. 78 ff.

STÜCKELBERGER, Christoph: *Umwelt und Entwicklung*, Stuttgart 1997, pp. 335–339.

Bericht aus Vancouver. Offizieller Bericht der Sechsten Vollversammlung des Ökumenischen Rates der Kirchen, Frankfurt 1983, p. 112.

3.11   Forgiveness

JAQUES, Geneviève: *Beyond Impunity. An Ecumenical Approach to Truth, Justice and Reconciliation*, Geneva 2000, pp. 34–52.

NORRIS, Kathleen: *Amazing Grace. A Vocabulary of Faith*, New York 1998, p. 150 f.

STÜCKELBERGER, Christoph: *Vermittlung und Parteinahme*, Zurich 1988, pp. 582–593.

MÜLLER-FAHRENHOLZ, Geiko: *Vergebung macht frei*, Frankfurt/M. 1996.

On Chapter 4: Instruments of ethical responsibility in trade

4.1   Planning instruments of business ethics

STEINMANN, Horst/KUSTERMANN, Brigitte: *Unternehmensethik und Management: Überlegungen zur Integration der Unternehmensethik in den Managementprozess*, HWE, vol. 3, pp. 210–231.

BLEICHER, Knut: *Unternehmungsphilosophie – Visionen und Missionen eines normativen Managements*, HWE, vol. 3, pp. 165–188.

Waxenberger, Bernhard: *Management der Unternehmensintegrität. Zertifizierung von ethisch orientiertem Wirtschaften* (doctoral thesis, working title; publication probably in 2002).

Müller-Hagedorn, Lothar: *Der Handel*, Stuttgart 1998, p. 151.

Thommen, Jean-Paul: *Managementorientierte Betriebswirtschaftslehre*, Zurich 6th ed., 1996, p. 107.

Dietzfelbinger, Daniel: *Aller Anfang ist leicht. Unternehmens- und Wirtschaftsethik für die Praxis*, 2nd ed., Munich 2000.

4.2   *The ethics of labelling 1: Survey*

4.3   *The ethics of labelling 2: Labelling provisions*
  → literature on chapters 4.4–4.7.

4.4   *The ethics of labelling 3: Brands*

Brun, M. (ed.): *Handelsmarken. Entwicklungstendenzen und Zukunftsperspektiven der Handelsmarkenpolitik*, Stuttgart, 2nd ed., 1997.

Brun, M.: *Die Marke. Symbolkraft eines Zeichensystems*, Berne 2000.

Müller-Hagedorn, L.: *Der Handel*, Stuttgart 1998, pp. 430–442.

Unverwüstliches System Markenartikel, Neue Zürcher Zeitung 24/25 June 2000, p. 27.

Bolz, N./Bosshart, D.: *Kultmarketing. Die neuen Götter des Marktes*, Düsseldorf 2nd ed., 1995.

Keller, Peter: *"Nescafé hat heute Kult-Charakter"*, Tages-Anzeiger, 31 Dezember 1999, p. 31.

4.5   *The ethics of labelling 4: Labels*

Bericht zur Umsetzung der Strategie des Bundesrates zur nachhaltigen Entwicklung, Massnahme No. 6 "Anerkennung und Förderung von Labels", Berne, February 2000.

Sozialgütesiegel. Werkzeuge für ethischen Handel. Ein von der New Economics Foundation für die Europäische Kommission erstellter Bericht, Brussels 1998 ("New Economics Foundation: Social Labels: Tools for Ethical Trade, prepared for the European Commission", Luxembourg 1998.)

4.6   *The ethics of labelling 5: Codes of conduct*

Europäische Kommission: *Verhaltenskodizes und Soziallabel. Ethischer Konsum und ethische Produktion*. Sondernummer von: *Der europäische soziale Dialog*, Brussels May 1999.

ILO: *Overview of Global Developments and Office Activities Concerning Codes of Conduct, Social Labelling and Other Private Sector Initiatives Addressing Labour Issues*, Geneva 1998.

OECD: *Codes of Corporate Conduct: An Inventory*, Paris 1999.

Misereor/Brot für die Welt/TransFair Deutschland (eds.): *Sozialsiegel und Verhaltenskodizes*, Cologne 2000.

Transparency International: *TI Reader on Codes of Conduct. A Sample Selection*, Berlin 1999.

TIEMANN, Regine: *Ethische Branchenstandards. Ein Lösungsweg für Unternehmen aus moralischen Dilemmata*, dnwe Schriftenreihe vol. 6, Munich 1999.

SIMMA, Bruno / HEINEMANN, Andreas: *Codes of Conduct*, HWE, vol. 2, pp. 403–418.

EGGER, Michel: *Codes de conduite des entreprises: place des producteurs, "empowerment" et positions du Sud*, in: INSTITUT UNIVERSITAIRE D'ETUDES DU DÉVELOPPEMENT IUED: *Commerce durable*, Geneva 2001, pp. 253–281.

Codes of Conduct. Sondernummer des *Asian Labour Update* No. 26, January 1998, Hongkong.

HEIDEL, Klaus: *Weder "Wunderwaffe" noch "zahnloser Tiger". Zehn Thesen zur Verständigung über die Relevanz von Verhaltenskodizes*, epd-Entwicklungspolitik No. 13 / 14, 1999, pp. 53–58.

TRIGO DE SOUSA, Inês: *Codes of Conduct and Monitoring Systems, Bangladesh Peoples's Solidarity Centre*, Amsterdam 2000.

4.7   The ethics of labelling 6: Controlling, monitoring

MÜLLER-HAGEDORN, Lothar: *Der Handel*, Stuttgart 1998, pp. 588–685.

WAXENBERGER, Bernhard: *Bewertung der Unternehmensintegrität. Grundlagen für die Zertifizierung eines ethisch orientierten Managements*, Institut für Wirtschaftsethik St. Gallen, *Beiträge und Berichte* No. 86, St. Gallen 1999.

NEW ECONOMICS FOUNDATION/CATHOLIC INSTITUTE FOR INTERNATIONAL RELATIONS (eds.): *Open Trading. Options for Effective Monitoring of Corporate Codes of Conduct. Executive Summary*, London 1997.

The same editors: *Monitoring Corporate Codes of Conduct. Discussion Paper*, 1996.

Keeping the Work Floor Clean. Monitoring Models in the Garment Industry. A Publication of the Clean Clothes Campaign, Amsterdam 1998.

REINHARD, Julyen: *Le monitoring indépendant. Etude pour Clean Clothes en Suisse*, Lausanne 1999.

CENTRE-INFO SUISSE (CI): *Méthode du CI d'analyse de la durabilité environnementale et sociale des entreprises*, Fribourg 1997.

INTERAGENCY GROUP ON BREASTFEEDING MONITORING: *Cracking the Code. Überwachung des internationalen Kodex zur Vermarktung von Muttermilchersatznahrung*, London/Stuttgart 1997.

TRIGO DE SOUSA, Inês: *Codes of Conduct and Monitoring Systems*, Bangladesh Peoples's Solidarity Centre, Amsterdam 2000.

STÜCKELBERGER, Christoph et al.: *Report of the Second Migros-Del Monte Social Clause Monitoring Panel*, Manila Nov. 1995.

4.8   Marketing ethics 1: Statistics

4.9   Marketing ethics 2: Communication and advertising

INTERNATIONAL CHAMBER OF COMMERCE ICC: *International Code of Advertising Practice*, 1997 ed., Paris.

SCHWEIZERISCHE LAUTERKEITSKOMMISSION: *Grundsätze. Lauterkeit in der kommerziellen Kommunikation,* Zürich 1998.

GÖBEL, Elisabeth: *Werbung,* HWE, vol. 4, pp. 648–670.

KAAS, Klaus Peter: *Ethische Aspekte der Werbung,* HWE, vol. 3, pp. 256–260.

ZIEGLER, Albert: *Verantwortung für das Wort. Kommunikation und Ethik,* Frauenfeld 2000.

4.10 *Marketing ethics 3: E-commerce*

BAROWSKI, Mike / MÜLLER, Achim: *Online-Marketing,* Berlin 2000.

UNCTAD: *E-Commerce and Development,* Geneva 2000.

Art. *Internet,* GLA, pp. 320–324.

Internet, e-commerce und das Exportgeschäft, Schweizer Aussenwirtschaft No. 57, July / August 2000, pp. 3–15.

KAISER, Helmut: *"Elektronische" Marktwirtschaft? Grundlegende Veränderungen durch den Electronic Commerce,* Zeitschrift für Evangelische Ethik, 45 / 2001, pp. 29–46.

JAEGGI, Urs: *Begrenzte grenzenlose Kommunikation. Im globalen Dorf lebt der Süden noch an der Peripherie,* Entwicklungspolitische Impulse No. 3 / 99, published by BROT FÜR ALLE, Berne 1999.

4.11 *Stakeholder ethics 1: Company ratings and stock-exchange indices*

Der Unternehmenstester. Die Lebensmittelbranche. Ein Ratgeber für den verantwortlichen Einkauf, Hamburg 1995.

COUNCIL ON ECONOMIC PRIORITIES: *The Corporate Report Card. Rating 250 of America's Corporations for the Socially Responsible Investor,* New York 1998.

COUNCIL ON ECONOMIC PRIORITIES: *Shopping for a Better World. The Quick and Easy Guide to all Your Socially Responsible Shopping,* San Francisco 1994.

WORLD ECONOMIC FORUM: ESI 2001 (Country Rating According to Environmental Criteria) → website: www.weforum.org.

4.12 *Stakeholder ethics 2: Campaigns*

CHAPMAN, Jennifer / FISHER, Thomas: *The Effectiveness of NGO Ccampaigning: Lessons from Practice,* Development in Practice, vol. 10, No. 2, May 2000, pp. 151–165.

4.13 *Stakeholder ethics 3: Boycotts and sanctions*

UNO: *Use of Sanctions under Chapter VII of the UN Charter,* Office of the Spokesman for the Secretary General OSSG (www.un.org/news/ossg/sanction. Constantly being updated).

4.14 *World trade policy 1: International conventions*

JAHRMANN, F.-Ulrich: *Aussenhandel,* Ludwigshafen 9th ed., 1998.

MÜLLER, Jörg, Paul / WILDHABER, Luzius: *Praxis des Völkerrechts* (particularly pp. 895-975: Grundzüge der Weltwirtschaftsordnung), 3rd ed., Berne 2001.

PETER, Hans-Balz: *"Kohärenz" als Kriterium für eine ethisch reflektierte Aussenpolitik,* Texte 10/95 des Instituts für Sozialethik des Schweizerischen Evangelischen Kirchenbundes, Berne 1995.

4.15 World trade policy 2: Social and environmental clauses

EGGER, Michel/SCHÜMPERLI, Catherine: *Clause sociale. Sondage auprès des ONG et syndicats européens et du Sud, série repères* No.1/96 de Pain pour le prochain, Lausanne 1996.

STÜCKELBERGER, Christoph: *Sozialklauseln im internationalen Handel. Wirtschaftsethische Kriterien, Schweizerische Zeitschrift für Aussenwirtschaft* 51st year, 1996, 75–100, as well as in Zeitschrift für Evangelische Ethik, 40th year, 1996, pp. 211–225.

STÜCKELBERGER, Christoph: *The Social Market Economy Needs International Social Clauses, Echo* (World Council of Churches, Geneva) No. 9, 1996, pp.12–14.

OECD: *Trade and Labour Standards. A Review of the Issues*, Paris 1995.

OECD: *Le commerce, l'emploi et les normes du travail. Une étude sur les droits fondamentaux des travailleurs et l'échange international*, Paris 1996.

WTO: *Annual Report* 1998, pp. 54–56.

LEISINGER, Klaus: *Wider die Versuchung der Erosion sozialer und ökologischer Standards auf Grund der Globalisierung*, in: PETER, Hans-Balz (ed.), *Globalisierung, Ethik und Entwicklung*, Berne/Stuttgart/Vienna 1999, pp. 89–102.

On Chapter 5: Agents of ethical responsibility in trade

5.1 A survey of agents

KIRCHNER, Christian: *Bedingungen interstaatlicher Institutionalisierung von wirtschaftlichen Prozessen*, HWE, vol. 2, pp.376–403.

5.2 Managers

ULRICH, Peter/THIELEMANN, Ulrich: *Ethik und Erfolg. Unternehmensethische Denkmuster von Führungskräften. Eine empirische Studie*, Berne/Stuttgart/Vienna 1992.

KAUFMANN, Franz-Xaver et al: *Ethos und Religion bei Führungskräften*, Munich 1986.

WITTMANN, Stephan: *Ethische Normen für das internationale Personalmanagement*, in: MAAK, Thomas/LUNAU, York (eds.): *Weltwirtschaftsethik*, Berne/Stuttgart/Vienna 1998, pp.401–422.

WITTMANN, Stephan: *Ethik und Personalmanagement*, Berne/Stuttgart 1998.

5.3 Gender: Women and men

WORLD BANK: *Sustainable Banking with the Poor. A Worldwide Inventory of Microfinance Institutions*, Washington 1996.

WORLD BANK: *World Development Report* 1999/2000, Washington 2000.

SOCIAL WATCH INITIATIVE: *Social Watch 2000*, Uruguay 2000, pp.79–88.

UNDP: *Bericht über die menschliche Entwicklung 2000*, Bonn 2000.

JOEKES SUSAN/WESTON, Ann: *Women and the New Trade Agenda*, UNIFEM, New York 1994.

FREY NAKONZ, Regula: *Geschlechterverhältnisse in der neoliberalen Entwicklung*, Entwicklungspolitische Impulse No. 2/98, published by BROT FÜR ALLE, Berne 1998.

Biesecker, Adelheid: *Vom Eigennutz zur Vorsorge – zukunftsfähiges Wirtschaften in der Weltgemeinschaft aus der Sicht einer feministischen Ökonomik*, in: Maak, Thomas/ Lunau, York (eds.), *Weltwirtschaftsethik*, Berne/Stuttgart/Vienna 1998, pp. 261–292.

Gähwiler, Claudia: *Auf dem Weg zu einem Frauen-Label?* Mosquito No. 8, 1996, p. 8.

Madörin, Mascha: *Die Ökonomie und der Rest der Welt. Überlegungen zur Problematik einer feministischen Politischen Ökonomie*, in: Diskussionskreis Frau und Wirtschaft (ed.), *Ökonomie weiterdenken! Beiträge von Frauen zu einer Erweiterung von Gegenstand und Methode*, Frankfurt and New York 1997.

5.4   *Company types 1: Transnational corporations*

UNCTAD: *World Investment Report 1999*, Geneva 1999.

UN Centre on Transnational Corporations: *Transnational Corporations in World Development*, New York 1988.

Anderson, Sarah/Cavanagh, John: *Top 200. The Rise of Global Corporate Power*, Corporate Watch, New York 2000.

Stiftung Entwicklung und Frieden: *Globale Trends 2000*, Frankfurt/M. 1999, pp. 208–211.

Razu, I. John Mohan: *Transnational Corporations as Agents of Dehumanisation in Asia. An Ethical Critique of Development*, Delhi 1999.

Stückelberger, Christoph: *Vermittlung und Parteinahme*, Zurich 1988, 549–575 (Dialogue between Churches and Transnational corporations).

De George, Richard T.: *Entrepreneurs, Multinationals and Business Ethics*, in: Enderle, Georges (ed.), *International Business Ethics. Challenges and Approaches*, Notre Dame 1999, pp. 271–280.

5.5   *Company types 2: Wholesale and retail trade (north)*

Rudolph, Thomas: *Erfolgreiche Geschäftsmodelle im europäischen Handel*, St. Gallen 2000.

OECD: *Small and Medium Enterprise*, Outlook: 2000 Edition.

Various trade statistics.

Statistisches Jahrbuch der Schweiz 2000, Zürich 1999.

Christian Aid: *The Global Supermarket. Britain's Biggest Shops and Food from the Third World*, London 1996.

Handwerk als Chance. Möglichkeiten einer gemeinwohlorientierten, sozialen und ökologischen Marktwirtschaft am Beispiel Handwerk. Eine Denkschrift der Evangelischen Kirche in Deutschland, Gütersloh 1997.

5.6   *Company types 3: Small producers/traders (south)*

ILO: *Key Indicators of the Labour Market*, Geneva 1999.

ILO: *Yearbook of Labour Statistics*, Geneva.

World Development Indicators 2000, pp. 50–53.

5.7   Company types 4: Informal sector

ILO: *Resolution Concerning Statistics of Employment in the Informal Sector*, Geneva January 1993.

ILO: *World Labour Report*, Geneva 1997.

HOLLEY, Heinz: *Informelle Wirtschaft oder die Ökonomie der Ausgrenzung*, in: ZAPOTOCZKY, Klaus / GRIEBL, Hildegard: *Weltwirtschaft und Entwicklungspolitik*, Frankfurt / M. 1996, pp. 58–73.

LANG, Eva: *Die Bedeutung des informellen Sektors in der Weltwirtschaft*, in: ZAPOTOCZKY, ibid., pp. 73–83.

5.8   Lobbyists 1: Shareholders

L'HÉLIAS, Sophie: *Le retour de l'actionnaire. Pratiques du corporate governance en France, aux Etats Unies et en Grande-Bretagne*, Paris 1997.

WENGER, Ekkehart / KNOLL, Leonhard: *Shareholder Value*, HWE, vol. 4, pp. 433–454.

Forschungsprogramm "Recht und Wirtschaftsethik", Teilprogramm "Aktionärsverantwortung" des Interdisziplinären Instituts für Ethik und Menschenrechte IIEDH an der Universität Fribourg / Schweiz.

Diverse Publikationen des Interfaith Centre on Corporate Responsibility ICCR, New York.

SCHNEIDER, J.-A.: *Le droit de l'actionnaire de proposer une résolution au vote de l'Assemblée générale*, manuscripts 30 / 3 / 1998.

5.9   Lobbyists 2: Employers' federations and chambers of commerce

GROSER, Manfred: *Ethische Aspekte wirtschaftsbezogenen Handelns von Interessenverbänden*, HWE, vol. 3, pp. 509–534.

MAYNTZ, R. (ed.): *Verbände zwischen Mitgliederinteressen und Gemeinwohl*, Gütersloh 1992.

5.10   Lobbyists 3: Trade unions and non-governmental organizations

INTERNATIONALER VERBAND FREIER GEWERKSCHAFTEN ICFTU: *Survey of Violations of Trade Union Rights*, Brussels 2000.

STIFTUNG ENTWICKLUNG UND FRIEDEN: *Globale Trends 2000*, Frankfurt / M. 1999.

VON AUER, Frank / SEGBERS, Franz (eds.), *Markt und Menschlichkeit. Kirchliche und gewerkschaftliche Beiträge zur Erneuerung der sozialen Marktwirtschaft*, Reinbek bei Hamburg 1995.

NUSCHELER, Franz / HAMM, Brigitte: *Die Rolle von NGO's in der internationalen Menschenrechtspolitik*, Bonn 1998.

WEISS, Thomas (ed.): *NGO's, the UN and Global Governance*, Boulder 1997.

UN NON-GOVERNMENTAL LIAISON SERVICE: *Handbook for NGO's of UN Agencies*, New York 1997.

FRIEDRICH-EBERT-STIFTUNG (ed.): *Globale Trends und internationale Zivilgesellschaft*, Bonn 1996.

5.11   Lobbyists 4: Fair-trade organizations
→ Literature on Chapter 6.8.

5.12   Religious communities and charities

Various authors: *Interdependenzen von Religion und Wirtschaft*, HWE, vol. 1, pp. 567–780.

Der christliche Glaube und die heutige Weltwirtschaft. Ein Studiendokument des Ökumenischen Rates der Kirchen, Geneva 1992 (translated into many languages).

Gemeinsam auf dem Weg. Offizieller Bericht der Achten Vollversammlung des Ökumenischen Rates der Kirchen, Harare 1998, Frankfurt/M. 1999.

KÜNG, Hans: *Weltethos für Weltpolitik und Weltwirtschaft*, Munich 1997.

VAN DEN BERG, Aart: *God and the Economy. Analysis and Typology of Roman Catholic, Protestant, Orthodox, Ecumenical and Evangelical Theological Documents on the Economy 1979–1992*, Delft 1998.

WEBLEY, Simon: *Values Inherent in the Interfaith Declaration of International Business Ethics*, in: ENDERLE, Georges (ed.), *International Business Ethics. Challenges and Approaches*, Notre Dame 1999, pp. 96–108.

STÜCKELBERGER, Christoph: *Vermittlung und Parteinahme. Der Versöhnungsauftrag der Kirchen in gesellschaftlichen Konflikten*, Zurich 1988, 549–575 (Dialogue between Churches and Business).

TAYLOR, Michael: *Not Angels but Agencies. The Ecumenical Response to Poverty*, London/Geneva 1995.

5.13   Networks for ethical business
→ Websites of the organizations that are mentioned.

Forum Wirtschaftsethik. Zeitschrift des Deutschen Netzwerks Wirtschaftsethik dnwe, Constance/Germany.

European Business Ethics Newsletter. Magazine of the European Business Ethics Network EBEN, Breukelen/Netherlands.

5.14   Standardization institutions

KIRCHNER, Christian: *Formen interstaatlicher Interaktionsregeln für wirtschaftliche Prozesse*, HWE, vol. 2, pp. 390–403.

EGGER, Monika: *ISO 21000 – SA 8000 – ILO – WTO*, Entwicklungspolitische Impulse Nr. 2/99, published by BROT FÜR ALLE, Berne 1999.

KÜNG, Hans: *Weltethos für Weltpolitik und Weltwirtschaft*, Munich 1997.

5.15   Accreditation institutions

For information about CEPAA/SA8000, → website www.cepaa.org.

5.16   Certification institutions

BECKER, Bernd: *Zertifizierung von Qualitätsmanagement-Systemen im Einzelhandel*, Frankfurt 1999.

BONUS, Holger (ed.): *Umweltzertifikate. Der steinige Weg zur Marktwirtschaft*, Berlin 1998.

KREFTER, Karl H. (ed.): *Europäisches Konzept für das Prüf- und Zertifizierungswesen*, Vienna 1994.

5.17 *Auditing institutions*

Annual reports of the five auditing and consulting firms mentioned.

PRICEWATERHOUSECOOPERS: *ValueReporting'*, New York 2000.

ROGERSON, Paul: *Credibility Gap (of the Big Five)*, International Accounting Bulletin 14, June 2000, p. 6 f.

Zügel für Revisoren. Neue Zürcher Zeitung, 8 August 2000.

BALLWIESER, Wolfgang / CLEMM, Hermann: *Wirtschaftsprüfung*, HWE, vol. 3, pp. 399–416.

REINHARD, Julyen: *Le monitoring indépendent*, Lausanne 1999 (study about various monitoring systems for Switzerland's Clean Clothes Campaign).

5.18 *Financing and insurance institutions*

JAHRMANN, Fritz-Ulrich: *Aussenhandel*, Ludwigshafen, 9th ed., 1998, pp. 405–499: The Financing of Foreign Trade.

KOSLOWSKI, Peter: *Ethik der Banken und der Börse. Finanzinstitutionen, Finanzmärkte, Insider-Handel*, Tübingen 1997.

ARGANDOÑA, Antonio (ed.): *The Ethical Dimension of Financial Institutions and Markets*, Berlin / New York / Tokyo 1995.

VAN LIEDEKERKE, Luc et al. (eds.): *Explorations in Financial Ethics*, Leuven 2000.

WEBER, Theo: *Globalisierung der Kapitalmärkte, ein Sachzwang für Unternehmen? Der Diskurs des internationalen Kapitals*, in: MAAK, Thomas / LUNAU, York (eds.), *Weltwirtschaftsethik*, Berne / Stuttgart / Vienna 1998, pp. 443-465.

STÜCKELBERGER, Christoph: *Fairer Handel mit Kapital. Übersicht, neue Ansätze, Perspektiven*. Entwicklungspolitische Impulse No. 3 / 1998, published by Brot für alle, Berne 1998.

PACHLATKO, Christoph: *Wertfragen im Management der Versicherung. Zur Rolle der Versicherung in der Wohlstandsgesellschaft*, St. Gallen 1988.

ACKERMANN, Walter: *Versicherung*, LWE, Sp. 1221–1227.

GRAF VON DER SCHULENBURG, Matthias: *Versicherungen*, HWE, vol. 4, pp. 633–647.

5.19 *Ethics advisory institutions*

LUNAU, York: *Unternehmensethikberatung*, Berne / Stuttgart / Vienna 2000.

KELLER, Christoph: *Hier spricht die Stimme der Vernunft. In der Schweiz boomen die Ethikkommissionen*, Tages-Anzeiger Magazin, 51 / 99, pp. 25–33.

5.20 *Nation-states*

Various authors: *Ethische Aspekte inner- und interstaatliche Institutionalisierung wirtschaftlicher Prozesse*, HWE, vol. 2, pp. 105–418.

EPPLER, Erhard: *Was braucht der Mensch? Politik im Dienst der Grundbedürfnisse*, Frankfurt / New York 2000, particularly pp. 92–117.

STIFTUNG ENTWICKLUNG UND FRIEDEN: *Globale Trends 2000*, Frankfurt / M. 1999, pp. 371–399.

5.21 *Supranational alliances of nations: Example: EU*

→ Websites with the documents of the EU, about the EU and trade, particularly http://europa.eu.in/comm/trade.

EUROPÄISCHE KOMMISSION: *Die Europäische Union und der Welthandel,* Brussels 1999.

KOMMISSION DER EUROPÄISCHEN GEMEINSCHAFTEN: *Mitteilung der Kommission an den Rat über den Fairen Handel,* Brussels 29/11/1999.

STRAHM, Rudolf: *Europaentscheid,* Zurich 1992.

5.22 *International organizations: Example: WTO*

INTERNATIONAL TRADE CENTRE/UNCTAD/WTO/COMMONWALTH SECRETARIAT: *Business Guide to the Uruguay Round,* Geneva 1995.

WTO: *Guide to GATT Law and Practice,* Geneva 1995.

HAUSER, Heinz/SCHANZ, Kai-Uwe: *Das neue Gatt. Die Welthandelsordnung nach Abschluss der Uruguay-Runde,* Munich 1995.

SENTI, Richard: *WTO. System und Funktionsweise der Welthandelsorganization,* Zurich 2000.

CHARNOVITZ, Steve: *The Moral Exception in Trade Policy,* Virginia Journal of International Law Association, vol. 38, 1998, pp. 689–746.

5.23 *International organizations: Example: ILO*

ILO: *ILO database on international labour standards,* 2000 (http://ilolex.ilo.ch).

Botschaften der Hoffnung. Inkrafttreten des IAO-Abkommens über die schlimmsten Formen der Kinderarbeit, Die Welt der Arbeit 37/2000, pp. 6–13.

→ documents of website www.ilo.org.

Defending Values, Promoting Change. Social Justice in a Global Economy: An ILO Agenda, Geneva 1994.

→ literature on chapters 4.6, 4.15, 5.7, 6.17.

5.24 *Global trade ethics under the conditions of a hegemonic power?*

FISCHER, Wolfram: *Internationale Ordnungssysteme unter den Bedingungen einer Hegemonialmacht,* HWE, vol. 2, pp. 418–433.

MAAK, Thomas/LUNAU, York (eds.): *Weltwirtschaftsethik,* Berne/Stuttgart/Vienna 1998, pp. 123–191 (essays on the demoncratic foundations of world trade).

On Chapter 6: Fields of action and tension

6.1 *Fair prices: Equilibrium and justice*

MÜLLER-HAGEDORN, Lothar: *Der Handel,* Stuttgart 1998, pp. 443–464.

EISENHUT, Peter: *Aktuelle Volkswirtschaftslehre,* Ausgabe 2000/2001, Chur/Zurich 2000, pp. 31–57.

KOSLOWSKI, Peter: *Prinzipien der Ethischen Ökonomie,* Tübingen 1988, pp. 262–303.

FEHL, U.: *Die Frage nach dem gerechten Preis,* in: GUTMANN, G./SCHÜLLER, A. (eds.), *Ethik und Ordnungsfragen der Wirtschaft,* Baden-Baden 1989, pp. 249–267.

Gerechter Preis? Materialien und Erwägungen zu einem entwicklungspolitischen und wirtschaftsethischen Problem, ISE-Beiträge 29, Berne 1990.

LIEBIG, Klaus/SAUTTER, Hermann: *Politische Wirkungen des Fairen Handels*, in: MISEREOR/BROT FÜR DIE WELT/FRIEDRICH-EBERT-STIFTUNG (eds.), *Entwicklungspolitische Wirkungen des Fairen Handels*, Aachen 2000, pp. 113–185, particularly pp. 120–125.

WEIZSÄCKER, Ernst U. von: *Erdpolitik*, Darmstadt 1990, pp. 143–159.

6.2   *Fair pay: Safeguarding people's existence*

Rerum Novarum (Social Encyclical by Pope Leo XIII, 1891), No. 34–35.

RIBHEGGE, Hermann: *Art. Lohn*, LWE, Sp. 616–624.

ILO: *Minimum Wage Fixing Convention*, 1970 (No. 131).

LÜPKES, Gerhard (ed.): *Über den Aussenhandel zwischen Ländern mit verschiedenem Lohnniveau. Eine Untersuchung über den Einfluss des Aussenhandels auf die Preise der Produktionsfaktoren*, Leer 1990.

THOMMEN, Jean-Paul: *Managementorientierte Betriebswirtschaftslehre*, Zurich, 6th ed., 1996.

6.3   *Fair speed: Adapted time*

STÜCKELBERGER, Christoph: *Umwelt und Entwicklung*, Stuttgart 1997, pp. 323–328 (the new measurement of time).

NADOLNY, S.: *Die Entdeckung der Langsamkeit*, Munich 1983.

HELD, M./GEISSLER, K. (eds.): *Ökologie der Zeit*, Tutzing 1993.

6.4   *Fair interest rates: The Reformer Calvin's rules*

CALVIN, Johannes: *Corpus Reformatorum C. R.*, vol. 38/I, p. 248f.

THIEL, Albrecht: *In der Schule Gottes. Die Ethik Calvins im Spiegel seiner Predigten über das Deuteronomium*, Neukirchen-Vluyn 1999, pp. 243–266.

Gerechter Preis? Materialien und Erwägungen zu einem entwicklungspolitischen und wirtschaftsethischen Problem, ISE-Beiträge 29, Berne 1990, pp. 70ff.

SEGBERS, Franz: *Die Hausordnung der Tora. Biblische Impulse für eine theologische Wirtschaftsethik*, Lucerne 2000, pp. 187ff, 383–399.

6.5   *Fair customs tariffs: Facilitating and steering trade*

IMF: *Revenue Implications of Trade Liberalization, Occasional Paper* No. 180, 1999.

→ literature about the following chapter 6.6, Fair taxation.

6.6   *Fair taxation: Sharing public costs*

SIEGEL, Theodor: *Steuern*, HWE, vol. 3, pp. 354–399.

Global Public Goods. Published for UNDP, ed. by Inge KAUL et al., New York 1999.

TANZI, Vito: *Is There a Need for a World Tax Organization? Paper Presented at the International Institute of Public Finance*, August 1996, Tel Aviv.

BALDWIN, Richard: *Globalisierung ohne Steuerharmonisierung*, Neue Zürcher Zeitung No. 175, 29/30 July 2000, p. 65.

CREUTZ, Helmut: *Wir brauchen ein anderes Steuersystem. Entwurf einer Alternative*, Aachen 1996.

STURM, Andreas et al.: *Die Gewinner und die Verlierer im globalen Wettbewerb. Warum Ökoeffizienz die Wettbewerbsfähigkeit stärkt. 44 Nationen im Test*, Chur/Zurich 1999.

RABUSHKA, Alvin/HALL, Robert: *The Flat Tax*, Stanford, 2nd ed., 1995.

6.7 *Fair profits: Fair attainment and distribution*

ULRICH, Peter: *Integrative Wirtschaftsethik*, Berne/Stuttgart/Vienna 1997, pp.397ff.

RICH, Arthur: *Wirtschaftsethik*, vol. 2, Güterlsoh 1990, pp.184f, 215f, 302f.

STÜCKELBERGER, Christoph: *Welcher Handel ist fair?* Entwicklungspolitische Impulse, No.1/97, Berne 1997, p.20f.

SEGBERS, Franz: *Die Hausordnung der Tora. Biblische Impulse für eine theologische Wirtschaftsethik*, Lucerne 2000, pp.375ff.

6.8 *Fair trade*

MISEREOR/BROT FÜR DIE WELT/FRIEDRICH-EBERT-STIFTUNG (eds.): *Entwicklungspolitische Wirkungen des Fairen Handels*, Aachen 2000.

European Fair Trade Association EFTA: Fair Trade Jahrbuch 1998–2000, Maastricht 1998.

EUROPÄISCHES PARLAMENT, *Ausschuss für Entwicklung und Zusammenarbeit: Bericht über Fairen Handel (Fassa Report)*, Brussels 26/5/1998.

Commission des Communautés Européennes: Communication de la Commission au Conseil sur le commerce équitable, Brussels 29/11/1999.

Schweizer Forum Fairer Handel: Grundsätze des Fairen Handels, Berne October 2000.

IUED: *Le commerce durable. Vers de plus justes pratiques commerciales entre le Nord et le Sud*, Geneva 2001.

STÜCKELBERGER, Christoph: *Welcher Handel ist fair?* Entwicklungspolitische Impulse No.1/97, Berne 1997.

COOTE, Belinda/OXFAM: *Der UnFaire Handel. Die "3. Welt" in der Handelsfalle und mögliche Auswege*, Stuttgart 1994.

6.9 *Unfair black-market trade*

SCHNEIDER, Friedrich/PÖLL, Günther: *Schattenwirtschaft*, HWE, vol. 4, pp.382–432.

SCHNEIDER, Friedrich: *Schwarzarbeit – Ursache oder Folge wirtschaftspolitischer Missstände?* Neue Zürcher Zeitung, 25/26 November 2000, p.101.

SCHNEIDER, Friedrich/ENSTE, Dominik: *Shadow Economies: Size, Causes and Consequences*, Journal of Economic Literature 38/1, 2000, pp.77–114.

→ literature on chapter 5.7, Informal sector.

6.10 *Unfair corruption*

PIETH, Mark/EIGEN, Peter (eds.): *Korruption im internationalen Geschäftsverkehr. Bestandsaufnahme, Bekämpfung, Prävention*, Neuwied 1999.

JAIN, Arvind K. (ed.): *Economics of Corruption*, Boston/Dordrecht/London 1998.

MAAK, Thomas/ULRICH, Peter: *Korruption – die Unterwanderung des Gemeinwohls durch Partikularinteressen. Eine republikanisch-ethische Perspektive*, in: PIETH, Mark/EIGEN, Peter (eds.), *Korruption im internationalen Geschäftsverkehr. Bestandsaufnahme, Bekämpfung, Prävention*, Luchterhand, Neuwied 1999, pp.103–119.

STÜCKELBERGER, Christoph: *Korruption bekämpfen. Eine drängende Aufgabe für Hilfs-werke, Missionen und Kirchen,* Berne 1999 (in English: *"Fighting Corruption. An Ur-gent Task for Aid Agencies, Missionary Societies and Churches",* Berne 1999; in French: *"Lutte contre la corruption. Une tâche urgente pour les oeuvres d'entraide, les missions et les Eglises",* Lausanne 2000).

KLEINER, Paul: *Bestechung. Eine theologisch-ethische Untersuchung,* Berne 1992.

TRANSPARENCY INTERNATIONAL: *Annual Report 1999* and homepage.

SHELL: *How Do We Stand. Report 2000.*

IUED (ed.): *Monnayer les pouvoirs. Espaces, mécanismes et représentations de la corrup-tion,* Paris 2000.

6.11   *Trade in information*

NETHÖFEL, Wolfgang: *Ethik zwischen Medien und Mächten.* Neukirchen-Vluyn 1999.

WIEGERLING, Klaus: *Medienethik,* Stuttgart 1998.

JAEGGI, Urs: *Begrenzte grenzenlose Kommunikation. Im globalen Dorf lebt der Süden noch an der Peripherie,* Entwicklungspolitische Impulse No. 3/99, Berne 1999.

Zeitschrift "Ethics and Information Technology", Kluwer Academic Publishers, 4 issues per year.

SJURTS, Ina: *Strategie der grössten Medienkonzerne der Welt,* in: HANS BREDOW-INSTITUT (ed.): *Internationales Jahrbuch für Hörfunk und Fernsehen,* Baden-Baden/Hamburg, pp. 28–38.

CULTURAL ENVIRONMENT MOVEMENT CEM: *The Cultural Environment Monitor* No. 1/ 1996, Philadelphia.

→ cf also e-commerce, chapter 4.10.

6.12   *Trade in raw materials*

WTO: *International Trade Statistics 2000,* Geneva 2000.

UNCTAD: *Trade and Development Report 2000,* Geneva 2000.

Die Jagd nach den Bodenschätzen. Umweltzerstörung und Menschenrechtsverletzungen im Süden als Folge von Rohstoffverschwendung im Norden, epd-Dritte-Welt-informa-tion No. 8–9/2000, Frankfurt/M.

6.13   *Trade in genetic technology*

WORLD BANK: *World Development Report 2000/2001,* Washington 2001.

LESSER, W./UNEP: *Institutional Mechanisms Supporting Trade in Genetic Materials,* Geneva 1994.

UNEP: *Access to Genetic Resources and Means for Fair and Equitable Benefit Sharing. Case Study submitted by Switzerland,* April 1998.

UNCTAD: *The TRIPs Agreement and Developing Countries,* Geneva 1996.

LEISINGER, Klaus M.: *Gentechnik für die Dritte Welt?* Basel 1991.

HÜBNER, Jürgen/VON SCHUBERT, Hartwig (eds.): *Biotechnologie und evangelische Ethik. Die internationale Diskussion,* Frankfurt/M./New York 1992.

CENTRE DE RECHERCHE POUR LE DÉVELOPPEMENT INTERNATIONAL: *Un brevet pour la vie. La propriété intellecuelle et ses effets sur le commerce, la biodiversité et le monde rural,* Ottawa 1994.

VAN AKEN, Jan: *Silent Death. The Possible Abuse of Genetic Engineering for Biological Warfare,* Echoes 18/2000, Geneva.

6.14   *Trade in capital 1: Ethical investments*

DAC/OECD: *Development Cooperation Report 1999,* table III/1.

LOOSLI, Hans-Peter: *Konsequenzen der Globalisierung für den Anleger,* UBS Investment May 2000, p.12f. Diagram from p.9.

WAGNER, Andreas: *Unternehmensethik in Banken,* Vienna 1999.

OBRIST, Philippe: *Wertorientierte Führung im Private Banking,* Berne 2000.

SCHNEEWEISS, Antje: *Mein Geld soll Leben fördern. Hintergrund und Praxis ethischer Geldanlagen,* Mainz/Neukirchen/Vluyn 1998.

DEML, Max et al.: *Rendite ohne Reue. Handbuch für die ethisch-ökologische Geldanlage,* Frankfurt/M. 1996.

DEML, Max/WEBER, Jörg: *Grünes Geld. Jahrbuch für ethisch-ökologische Geldanlagen 2000/2002,* Munich 2000.

STÜCKELBERGER, Christoph: *Fairer Handel mit Kapital,* Entwicklungspolitische Impulse No.3/98, Berne 1998.

BROT FÜR ALLE/FASTENOPFER/INSTITUT FÜR SOZIALETHIK/JUSTITITA ET PAX: *Verantwortlich Geld anlegen. Ein ethischer Leitfaden für Kirchgemeinden und Privatpersonen,* Berne 2001.

ERKLÄRUNG VON BERNE/WWF: *Ethisch-ökologische Geldanlagen in der Schweiz. Einführung, Handlungsvorschläge, Marktübersicht,* EvB-Dok 6/2000, Zurich 2000.

6.15   *Trade in capital 2: Foreign currency trade and speculation*

TOBIN, James: *A Proposal for International Monetary Reform,* in: *Eastern Economic Journal,* vol.4, 1978, pp.153–159.

EICHENGREEN, Barry/TOBIN, James/WYPLOSZ, Charles (1995): *Two Cases for Sand in the Wheels of International Finance,* The Economic Journal, vol.105, No.428, 1995, pp.162–172.

SCHMIDT, Rodney: *A Feasible Foreign Exchange Transactions Tax,* North-South Institute, Canada, March 1999.

SPAHN, Paul Bernd: *International Financial Flows and Transactions Taxes: Survey and Options,* IMF Working Paper WP 95/60, Washington D.C. 1995.

BODE, Bart: *Currency Transaction Tax: A Domestic Resource for Social and Sustainable Development. Paper Presented on behalf of CIDSE and Caritas Internationalis, NGO Hearings at the High Level Intergovernmental Event on Financing for Development,* New York, 6 November 2000.

BELLO, Walden / BULLARD, Nicola / MALHOTTA, Kamal (eds.): *Global Finance. New Thinking on Regulating Speculative Capital Markets*, London / New York 2000.

JAHRMANN, F.-Ulrich: *Aussenhandel*, Ludwigshafen, 9th ed., 1998, pp. 305ff.

KOSLOWSKI, Peter: *Ethik der Banken und der Börse*, Tübingen 1997.

VAN LIEDEKERKE, Luc: *Currency Crisis, Tobin Tax and International Justice*, in: VAN LIEDEKERKE, Luc et al. (eds.), *Explorations in Financial Ethics*, Leuven 2000, pp. 173–204.

BOATRIGHT, John R.: *Ethics in Finance*, Blackwell 1999.

Kapital braucht Kontrolle. Die internationalen Finanzmärkte: Funktionsweise, Alternativen, hrsg. von Kairos Europa / WEED, Heidelberg / Bonn 2000.

SPAHN, P. B.: *Die Tobin-Steuer und die Stabilität der Wechselkurse*, Finanzierung und Entwicklung 33 (2), pp. 24ff.

RAFFER, Kunibert: *The Tobin Tax. Reviving a Discussion*, World Development 26 (3), 1998.

BROT FÜR ALLE (ed.): *The Tobin Tax. Three Studies from the South*, Berne 2001.

6.16 *Trade in capital 3: Debt ethics*
WORLD BANK: *Global Development Finance 2000*, vol. 1, *Analysis and Summary Tables*, Washington 2000, p. 188.

PETER, Hans-Balz et al.: *Kreative Entschuldung*, ISE-Diskussionsbeiträge 30, Berne 1990.

SCHMID-HOLZ, Daniel: *Schuld und Schulden. Die Perspektive des Leidens unter der Schuldenkrise im Konflikt mit dem Courant normal des Schuldenmanagements*, ISE-Diskussionsbeiträge No. 31, Berne 1991.

6.17 *Trade and jobs*
ILO: *World Employment Report 2001*, Geneva 2001.

WTO: *International Trade Statistics 2000*, Geneva 2000.

CORPORATE WATCH (Sarah ANDERSON / John CAVANAGH): *Top 200: The Rise of Global Corporate Power*, New York 2000.

DRITTE WELT-INFORMATION: *Weltmarkt für Arbeitskraft. Migrationsbewegungen in der globalen Weltwirtschaft*, No. 3–4 / 2000.

LANG, Eva: *Die Bedeutung des informellen Sektors* → literature on chapter 5.7.

Les églises protestantes et la question sociale. Positions oecuméniques sur la justice sociale et le monde du travail, BIT / ILO, Geneva 1996.

ARN, Christof: *HausArbeitsEthik. Strukturelle Probleme und Handlungsmöglichkeiten rund um die Haus- und Familienarbeit in sozialethischer Perspektive*, Chur / Zurich 2000.

6.18 *Trade and human rights*
Principles for the Conduct of Company Operations within the Oil and Gas Industry (with particular emphasis on ecologically and socially sensitive areas). A Discussion Paper, published by BREAD FOR THE WORLD, Stuttgart 2000.

AVERY, Christopher, L.: *Business and Human Rights in a Time of Change*, Amnesty International, London 2000.

ADDO, Michael (ed.): *Human Rights Standards and the Responsibility of Transnational Corporations*, Dordrecht/Boston/London 1999.

BRASSEL, Frank/WINDFUHR, Michael: *Welthandel und Menschenrechte*, Bonn 1995.

BLANKART, Franz: *Handel und Menschenrechte. Vortrag an der Konferenz der Schweizer Botschafter 1995* (manuscript), Berne 1995.

6.19   Trade and cultures: Intercultural management

LANGE, Heiko et al. (eds.): *Working Across Cultures. Ethical Perspectives for Intercultural Management*, Dordrecht/Boston/London 1998.

ENDERLE, Georges (ed.): *International Business Ethics*, Notre Dame/London 1999.

PALAZZO, Bettina: *Interkulturelle Unternehmensethik. Deutsche und amerikanische Modelle im Vergleich*, Wiesbaden 2000.

Interkulturelles Management: Unverzichtbar im Export. Dossier mit verschiedenen Artikeln, Schweizer Aussenwirtschaft No. 50, December 1999.

BUJO, Bénézet: *Kulturelle Perspektiven für eine Ethik der Entwicklung im Prozess der Globalisierung*, in: PETER, Hans-Balz (ed.), *Globalisierung, Ethik und Entwicklung*, Berne/Stuttgart 1999, pp. 123–131.

KRAMER, Dieter: *Eine Ressource für Zukunftsfähigkeit. Die Debatte um Kultur und Entwicklung nach der Stockholmer UNESCO-Konferenz*, epd-Entwicklungspolitik No. 12/1998, pp. 29–32.

KOFI APPIAH, Simon: *Africanness, Inculturation, Ethics. In Search of the Subject of an Inculturated Christian Ethic*, Frankfurt/M. 2000.

6.20   Trade and religions: Interfaith management

KOTKIN, Joel: *Stämme der Macht. Der Erfolg weltweiter Clans in Wirtschaft und Politik*, Reinbek bei Hamburg 1996 (English original: *"How Race, Religion and Identity Determine Success in the New Global Economy"*, New York 1992).

WEBLEY, Simon: *Values Inherent in the Interfaith Declaration of International Business Ethics*, in: ENDERLE, Georges (ed.), *International Business Ethics*, Notre Dame/London 1999, pp. 98–108.

KÜNG, Hans: *Weltethos für Weltpolitik und Weltwirtschaft*, Munich 1997.

WELTBANK: *World Faith Development Dialogue*, diverse Dokumente für den *World Development Report* 2000/2001 der Weltbank.

6.21   Trade and peace

International Institute for Strategic Studies: The Military Balance 1998/99, London 1998, p. 270.

KÜNG, Hans: *Weltfrieden durch Religionsfrieden*, Munich 1993.

SENGHAAS, Dieter: *Geokultur: Wirklichkeit oder Fiktion? Drei Abhandlungen zur Debatte über den "Zusammenprall der Zivilisationen"*, Arbeitspapiere der Schweiz. Friedensstiftung No. 21, Berne 1995.

Rüstungsproliferation und Konversion: Sektoranalysen (various essays), in: Büttner, Veronika/Krause, Joachim (eds.), *Rüstung statt Entwicklung? Sicherheitspolitik, Militärausgaben und Rüstungskontrolle in der Dritten Welt,* Baden-Baden 1995, 23–127 und 611–702.

Bächler, Günther et al.: *Umweltzerstörung: Krieg oder Kooperation? Ökologische Konflikte im internationalen System und Möglichkeiten der friedlichen Bearbeitung,* Münster 1993.

6.22 *Ethical trade: Symbol and market power*

Misereor/Brot für die Welt/Friedrich-Ebert-Stiftung (eds.): *Entwicklungspolitische Wirkungen des Fairen Handels,* Aachen 2000.

Utting, Peter/UNRISD: *Business Responsibility for Sustainable Development,* UNRISD Occasional Paper 2, January 2000.

6.23 *Morals provide capital*

Leisinger, Klaus: *Unternehmensethik,* Munich 1997, pp. 175–191.

Thielemann, Ulrich/Breuer, Markus: *Ethik zahlt sich langfristig aus – stimmt das?* Forum Wirtschaftsethik, 2/2000, pp. 8-13.

Freisberg, Alexander: *Wunderwaffe Ethik. Immer mehr Unternehmen setzen auf Ethikschulungen, um ihrem wachsenden Wirtschaftskriminalitätsproblem zu begegnen,* Handelsblatt 23.6.2000, K4.

Internet addresses

The list contains those institutions which are mentioned in the book.

AA   Institute for Social and Ethical AccountAbility, London
www.accountability.org.uk

Aprodev   Association of Protestant Development Organizations in Europe
www.oneworld.org/aprodev

ATTAC   Association pour une Taxation des Transactions financières
pour l'Aide aux Citoyens
www.attac.org

AW   Arthur Andersen (Worldwide)
www.arthurandersen.com

Basler Abfallentsorgungskonvention
www.basel.int

BIODIV   Biodiversitätskonvention
www.biodiv.org

BFA   Brot für Alle, Switzerland
www.bfa-ppp.ch

BfdW   Brot für die Welt, Germany
www.brot-fuer-die-welt.de

BWI   Bread for the World, USA
www.bread.org

CA   Christian Aid, UK
www.christian-aid.org.uk

CCA   Christian Conference of Asia
www.cca.org.hk

CCC   Clean Clothes Campaign
www.cleanclothes.org

CCEE   Council of European Bishops' Conferences
www.kath.ch/ccee

CENELEC   European Committee for Electrotechnical Standardization
www.cenelec.org

CI   Centre Info Fribourg, Switzerland
www.centreinfo.ch

CIDSE   International Cooperation for Development and Solidarity
www.cidse.org

CIIR   Catholic Institute for International Relations, UK
ww.ciir.org

CLAI   Consejo Latinoamericano de Iglesias
www.ecuanex.apc.org/clai

CSR	Corporate Social Responsibility Europe	
	www.csreurope.org	
DJSGI	Dow Jones Sustainability Group Index	
	www.sustainability-index.com	
DNWE	Deutsches Netzwerk Wirtschaftsethik	
	www.dnwe.de	
DTT	Deloitte Touche Tohmatsu	
	www.deloitte.com	
EA	Ernst & Young International	
	www.ey.com	
EAALCE	Ecumenical Association of Academies and Lay Centres in Europe	
	www.eaalce.de	
EAO	Ethics Officer Association	
	www.eoa.org	
EBEN	European Business Ethics Network	
	www.eben.org	
ETI	Ethical Trading Initiative, UK	
	www.ethicaltrade.org	
ETSI	European Telecommunication Standards Institute	
	www.etsi.org	
EU	European Union	
	http://europa.eu.int	
FLO	Fairtrade Labelling Organizations International	
	www.fairtrade.net	
FSC	Forest Stewardship Council International	
	www.fsc-deutschland.de	
GC	Global Compact (UNO)	
	www.unglobalcompact.org	
GDN	Global Development Network	
	www.gdnet.org	
GP	Global Policy Forum New York	
	www.globalpolicy.org	
GPG	Global Public Goods	
	www.undp.org/globalpublicgoods	
IABS	International Association for Business & Society	
	www.iabs.net	
IASC	International Accounting Standards Committee	
	www.iasc.org.uk	
ICC	International Chamber of Commerce	
	www.icc.org	

ICCR	Interfaith Centre on Corporate Responsibility
	www.iccr.org
ICFTU	International Confederation of Free Trade Unions
	www.icftu.org
ICTSD	Internatonal Centre for Trade and Sustainable Development
	www.ictsd.org
IFAT	International Federation for Alternative Trade
	www.ifat.org
ILO	International Labour Organization
	www.ilo.org
Infostelle für Umwelt- und Soziallabels, Switzerland	
	www.umweltschutz.ch/labelinfo
ISBEE	International Society of Business, Economics and Ethics
	www.isbee.org
ISE	Institut für Sozialethik, Berne, Switzerland
	www.ref.ch/ise
ISO	International Organization for Standardization
	www.iso.ch
IP	Iustitia et Pax Europa
	www.jupax-eu.org
IWE	Institut für Wirtschaftsethik, University of St. Gallen, Switzerland
	www.iwe.unisg.ch
IWF	International Monetary Fund
	www.imf.org
JPCH	Schweizerische Nationalkommission Justitia et Pax
	www.kath.ch/juspax
Jub	Jubilee 2000
	www.jubilee2000uk.org
KEK	Conference of European Churches
	www.cec-kek.org
KPMG	KPMG International
	www.kpmg.com
LMC	International Campaign to Ban Landmines
	www.icbl.org
NEWS	Network of European World Shops
	www.worldshops.org
NSW	Netzwerk für sozial verantwortliche Wirtschaft, Switzerland
	www.nsw-rse.ch

PWC	PricewaterhouseCoopers
	www.pwcglobal.com
SAI	Social Accountability International
	www.sa-intl.org
SC	South Centre Geneva
	www.southcentre.org
SGS	Société générale de surveillance
	www.sgs.com
Shell	Firma Shell
	www.shell.com/integrity
TI	Transparency International
	www.transparency.de
TWN	Third World Network
	www.twnside.org.sg
UNCTAD	United Nations Conference on Trade and Development
	www.unctad.org
UNDP	United Nations Development Programme
	www.undp.org
UNEP	United Nations Environmental Programme
	www.unep.org
UNFCC	United Nations Framework Convention on Climate Change
	www.unfccc.de
UNO	United Nations
	www.un.org
	Verband der Schweizer Unternehmen
	www.economiesuisse.ch
WB	World Bank
	www.worldbank.org
WBCSD	World Business Council for Sustainable Development
	www.wbcsd.org
WCC	World Council of Churches
	www.wcc-coe.org
WEF	World Economic Forum
	www.weforum.org
WTO	World Trade Organization
	www.wto.org

Index